TENNYSON

TENNYSON

BY

ARTHUR CHRISTOPHER BENSON

FOURTH EDITION

BOOKS FOR LIBRARIES PRESS
FREEPORT, NEW YORK

First Published 1913
Reprinted 1970

INTERNATIONAL STANDARD BOOK NUMBER:
0-8369-5570-6

LIBRARY OF CONGRESS CATALOG CARD NUMBER:
76-137369

PRINTED IN THE UNITED STATES OF AMERICA

PREFACE

THE object of this little book is threefold; I have tried (1) to give a simple narrative of the life of Tennyson, with a sketch of his temperament, character, ideals and beliefs; (2) I have tried from his own words and writings to indicate what I believe to have been his view of the poetical life and character; (3) I have attempted to touch the chief characteristics of his art from the technical point of view, here again as far as possible using his own recorded words.

My aim has been not to deal largely in quotation, but to take for granted a knowledge of the works, and if possible to send a reader back to them.

I am, of course, deeply indebted to the present Lord Tennyson's great *Memoir*, which, for all its tender simplicity of form, is a perfect mine of interest and pleasure; and I here acknowledge very gratefully the kind permission which Lord Tennyson readily gave me to make use of his book,[1] and even

---

[1] I may here also record my obligation to my sister, Miss Margaret Benson, to Mr. Edmund Gosse, and to Mr. F. R. B. Duff for valuable assistance, criticism and advice.

to reproduce certain of the illustrations. I have read and re-read the poems; I have studied several critical volumes; I have talked with friends of the Poet; with himself to my eternal regret I never exchanged a word. *Virgilium vidi tantum!*

It will thus be seen that I claim neither novelty of view nor elaborate apparatus of learning; but my work is based on admiration and reverent love, and the desire to share with others an inheritance of pure and deep delight.

A. C. B.

AUTHORITIES

*N*O *biography of the first Lord Tennyson can be named in the same day with that published, in 1897, in two volumes, by his son, the second Lord. In the course of the present work my indebtedness to this rich store of material is patent. Until the publication of this official* Life, *the most important studies in the biography of Tennyson were the charming* Records, *by Mrs. Thackeray Ritchie, and the painstaking and critical* Life *by Mr. Arthur Waugh, each published in 1892. The volumes by Hallam, Lord Tennyson, rendered both of these earlier compilations in the main obsolete, yet each contains material not found in the larger* Memoir. *In* 1898 *the Master of the Temple (Dr. Alfred Ainger) produced a valuable summary of Tennyson's career in the* Dictionary of National Biography. *Other monographs of more or less value call for no special reference here, but it should be added that, since the following pages were written, a volume, mainly critical, dealing with Tennyson, has been published by Mr. Andrew Lang* (1901) ; *and a monograph, biographical and critical, in the* English Men of Letters *series, by Sir Alfred Lyall* (1902).

The great importance of comparing the early texts of Tennyson with one another was earliest perceived by the late Mr. J. Dykes Campbell, who, in 1862, *printed the early text of the poems later rewritten, in a small volume entitled* Poems MDCCCXXX-MDCCCXXXIII, *which was issued anonymously and almost surreptitiously, in reference to Tennyson's known sensitiveness on the subject. The peculiarities of these texts were further dwelt upon by the late Mr. Richard Herne Shepherd in his* Tennysoniana *of* 1866 (*enlarged in* 1879 *and again in* 1896). *They have been made the subject of still fuller examination by Mr. J. Churton Collins in his* Early Poems of Alfred Tennyson, 1900, *to which reference has been made in the following pages.*

ALFRED TENNYSON

CHAPTER I

ALFRED TENNYSON was born in 1809, a year that, as Homer says, was "ἀγαθὴ κουρότροφος" "a goodly nurse of heroes." [1]   He came of a stock of Lincolnshire landed gentry.   He was descended through his grandmother from John, Earl Rivers, and on his father's side from a vigorous and puritanical race of yeomen.   His grandfather, George Tennyson of Bayons Manor, was an M.P. and a large land-owner, but the Poet's father, though he was the eldest son, had been disinherited in favour of his younger brother, who assumed the name of d'Eyncourt. Alfred was the fourth of twelve children, eight sons and four daughters.   Two of his brothers, Frederick and Charles,—the latter of whom inherited the name of Turner with a small estate,—attained to eminence as poets.   Ten of the family reached a patriarchal age, which testifies to the extraordinary physical vigour of the race.   "The Tennysons never die,"

[1] In 1809 were born Mendelssohn, Darwin, Abraham Lincoln, Oliver Wendell Holmes, FitzGerald and Gladstone.

said one of them, at a moment when death seemed the one thing to be desired.

The Poet's father was a man of strong character and imperious temper, with a deep vein of morbid melancholy, an inheritance from which his children did not entirely escape; his dark moods often over-shadowed the family circle with severity and in-justice, and caused Alfred, as a boy, hours of bewildered depression. Charles Tennyson Turner, writing in 1831 of his father's death, said that his father, "a man of sorrow and acquainted with grief," had been "on earth daily racked by bitter fancies and tossed about by strong troubles." "My father," he once said, "almost mocked at our attempts (to write poetry), although he used himself to write verses;" but he also records how he and his brother Alfred used to read their verses to his mother as they went slowly through green lanes, she in her chair, drawn by a great mastiff, her boys beside her. "Oh," he said, "all that there is of good and kind in any of us came from her tender heart!"

Though the family seems to have been Danish in origin, there was evidently a strong strain of dark southern blood in them, perhaps derived from a Huguenot ancestress. "Macaulay was afraid of you," said Carlyle, with a loud guffaw, to Tennyson, when the latter had described a highly unsatisfactory interview with the historian, "you are such a black man." Alfred was often taken for a foreigner in later life, and the portrait of Charles exhibits something of a Semitic cast of feature, and is like a wise and kindly Rabbi. "I am black-blooded," the Poet used to say, "like all the Tennysons." He no doubt used this expression with a primary allusion to his superficial appearance, but with an ultimate reference to the hereditary melancholy which characterised the family.

There is a charming legend, which, it is said, D. G. Rossetti used to relate with infinite gusto, of a guest being invited to dine at a certain house in London and arriving early; he was shown into an apparently deserted drawing-room, and while he was occupying the moments in the uneasy and self-regarding pastimes characteristic of such a situation, a gigantic dark man rose with a heavy sigh from the rug in front of the fire where he had been reclining in full evening dress, saying, "I must introduce myself: I am Septimus, the most morbid of the Tennysons." Grotesque as the story is, it is a humorous illustration of what was a far from humorous inheritance for the family.

Alfred was born on the 6th of August, 1809, at his father's rectory of Somersby in Lincolnshire. According to the fashion of the times Dr. Tennyson held three other preferments, but resided at Somersby, in a quaint rambling house, with later Gothic additions, the most conspicuous being a large dining-room with stained glass in the windows, that cast, as Charles said, "butterfly souls" on the walls.

Somersby lies on the edge of a wold, in a county of low, large, grey hillsides, great pastures, and quiet villages noted for their high-towered churches. Not far away was Mablethorpe, with its wide sea-marshes and low sand-dunes, where the long breakers fall with a heavy clap and spread in a curdling blanket of seething foam over the level sands. The scene of his birth was commemorated by the Poet in the *Ode to Memory* and in the Song *A Spirit haunts;* and through the whole of his works are to be found similes and nature-pictures drawn from the surroundings of his childhood with a luxuriant precision of detail that only the undimmed faculty of childish observation could supply. About Tennyson there clung to the end of his life a noble and undefinable flavour of the soil that recalls the "rusticitas" of Virgil, an impatience of towns, an absorbing passion for the open air, an independence of weather, a love of the seclusion of wild and woodland places. Moreover, the ceremonious dress and the conventional usages of society oppressed and bewildered him; and in his stately gruffness of address, his uncouth movements, and his rich Doric pronunciation, the country product was unmistakably to be seen.

The "legend," so to speak, of the early days is rich in characteristic touches. We hear how the boy, on hearing of Byron's death, "a day when the whole world seemed to be darkened for me," carved the words, "Byron is dead," on a sandstone rock by the secluded spring of Holywell; how he sat at his window to watch the golden globes of the apples lying in the orchard grass; how he called a young owl to his window, and tamed it. How of Louth School, where he went at the age of seven, and which he hated bitterly, he retained no pleasurable thought but the memory of the words *sonus desilientis aquae* and the sight of an old wall covered with wild weeds; how certain phrases haunted his childish brain with echoes of strange beauty; how, walking with his brother in the woods, he said, "I mean to be famous."

What especially appealed to his sensitive spirit was the presence of water in all its forms; the full stream lost in a tangle of rich water-plants, or fretting over the gravel; the welling up of silent springs; the face of woodland pools with their black depths; the sound and movement of the sea; and further, from his earliest days, astronomical ideas possessed a peculiar fascination for him. His Cambridge note-books were scrawled over with astronomical diagrams. He fed on the thought of the infinite spaces sown with star-dust, even recommending the thought to a brother as a cure for shyness.

As he wrote in a stanza which he afterwards

rejected for the *Palace of Art* as a "workshop chip," he was haunted by the thought of

> Regions of lucid matter taking forms,
>   Brushes of fire, hazy gleams,
> Clusters and beds of worlds, and bee-like swarms
>   Of suns, and starry streams.

He accused himself in an early letter to a relation of being volatile and fickle. But others said of him that though abstracted and moody he was always kind and good-tempered—"he never quarrelled."

His education was desultory; he was taught at first by his father; at school he learnt enough of the classics to make it possible for him to read them easily and with intense appreciation; but he was a scholar more in the liberal than in the technical sense.

From the first he knew the sweet magic of words; he took delight in melodious collocations, and musical phrases hummed in the childish brain; one of his earliest attempts at writing was to cover a slate with a poem in the style of Thomson, which was shown to his elder brother. "Yes, you can write," was the answer, as the slate was gravely handed back. Between the age of fifteen and seventeen he wrote in conjunction with his brother Charles a little volume which was published by a bookseller, Jackson of Louth, under the title of *Poems by two Brothers*. A few of their eldest brother Frederick's pieces were included. They received the liberal sum of £20, but had to take half in books from Mr. Jackson's shop. Some other poems of a slightly earlier date exist, published in the *Memoir*. One of these, called *The Coach of Death*, shows an extraordinary power of heaping up grotesque detail. As Jowett said, when he was shown these poems, " It is wonderful how the whelp can have known such things." On the afternoon of publication the two boys hired a carriage, and driving over to Mablethorpe "shared their triumph with the winds and waves."

In 1828 Alfred matriculated with his brother Charles at Trinity College, Cambridge. The elder brother Frederick was already in residence and had won some reputation as a scholar.

The two brothers at first occupied rooms at 12 Rose Crescent, and afterwards in King's Parade, nearly opposite St. Catherine's College, at No. 57 Corpus Buildings. Tennyson did not take at all kindly to Cambridge at first sight. "The country," he wrote to his aunt, "is so disgustingly level, the revelry of the place so monotonous, the studies of the University so uninteresting, so much matter of fact. None but dry-headed, calculating, angular little gentlemen can take much delight in them."

Tennyson produced a great impression at Cambridge from the first by his magnificent presence, his splendid face, the nobly poised head, with dark wavy hair, and the strong finely modelled hands.

"That man must be a poet," said Thompson, afterwards Master of Trinity, on seeing Tennyson come into Hall as an undergraduate. The circle with whom he became intimate was a remarkable one. There was the mild and sapient Spedding, the most unselfish and loving of men, who was to devote his career to the *Life of Bacon*, "re-editing works which did not want any such re-edition and vindicating a character which could not be cleared," as FitzGerald too incisively wrote. There was Monckton Milnes, afterwards Lord Houghton, an accomplished patron of literature; Trench, the poet, afterwards Archbishop of Dublin; Alford, afterwards Dean of Canterbury and the writer of noble hymns; Blakesley, a dry and caustic scholar, afterwards Dean of Lincoln; Merivale, the historian, afterwards Dean of Ely; and Arthur Hallam, son of the historian, by universal testimony the most brilliant genius of that brilliant group, the "master-bowman" of debate. "He was as near perfection as mortal man could be," wrote Tennyson of him. Edward Fitz-Gerald did not know Tennyson at Cambridge, which is to be regretted, because FitzGerald had a genius for remembering and noting salient characteristics; and his later memoranda of Tennyson are the most interesting and vivid of all the biographical records of him.

At Cambridge Tennyson read in a desultory way classics, history and science. He was noted among his friends for a certain Johnsonian gravity and common sense, a rich vein of humour, geniality combined with shyness; but he was oppressed at times with "moods of misery unutterable." He was an early member of a secret debating society called the Apostles, which discussed social, political and literary topics. The tendency of thought among the rising young men of the time was a hopeful and idealistic Radicalism, a hatred of ignorance and stagnation, a sympathy for the downtrodden and miserable, a dislike of parties and sects; and a firm belief that the world had only to be educated and enlightened to burst into an era of progress and amelioration. The mistake, as Blakesley pointed out in a letter to Tennyson in 1830, made by the young Radicals of Cambridge, was that they thought, with Shelley, that Society could be reformed by the suppression of institutions that led to tyranny and selfishness; and only learnt later that, as Wordsworth taught, no real reformation could be arrived at except by a guiding and transforming principle developed from within. The society exercised a deep influence on its members by what Carlyle in the *Life of Sterling* called its "ingenuous collision." [1] Tennyson had a habit of musing intently at the meetings, uttering oracular and judicial sayings at intervals. He professed himself too shy to read

[1] For a description of one of these meetings, *v. In Memoriam*, lxxxvii.

B

papers; and there is no doubt that his nervous organisation was even then painfully sensitive.

In 1829 he won the Chancellor's English Medal by a blank verse poem on Timbuctoo. It was not even written for the prize, but was an old poem on the *Battle of Armageddon*, with alterations and additions. It is a strange rhapsodical piece, with splendid imaginative power and full of pictorial splendour and sonorous lines; a short passage may be quoted:—

> I saw
> The smallest grain that dappled the dark earth,
> The indistinctest atom in deep air,
> The moon's white cities, and the opal width
> Of her small glowing lakes, her silver heights
> Unvisited with dew of vagrant cloud,
> And the unsounded, undescended depth
> Of her black hollows.

It is much to the credit of the examiners that they gave the prize to so original a poem, so removed from ordinary academical standards and with such scanty reference to the subject set. It was, moreover, composed in blank verse, and not in the heroic couplets up to that time considered *de rigueur* in this competition. There is a legend that the poem was not really recommended for the prize, but that the examiners' comments were misunderstood; this, however, rests on inadequate authority. Tennyson was too shy to deliver his poem in the Senate House, but entrusted the task to his friend Merivale.

Tennyson, like Dryden, did not in after life regard Cambridge with any particular affection or gratitude.

Such advantages as he had gained there he owed, he believed, to stimulating companionship, not to the direct academical influences of the place.   In a fine denunciatory sonnet, entitled *Lines on Cambridge of* 1830, he says that all the rich and ancient beauties of Cambridge shall not avail her when "the Daybeam" shall arise over England :—

> because your manner sorts
> Not with this age wherefrom ye stand apart,
> Because the lips of little children preach
> Against you, you that do profess to teach
> And teach us nothing, feeding not the heart.

In 1830 Tennyson undertook with Hallam a remarkable and romantic task.   A revolution had lately broken out in the Pyrenees under Torrijos, a high-minded revolutionist, against the Inquisition, and the tyranny of King Ferdinand II.   Hallam and Tennyson went off to Spain, and held a secret meeting on the Spanish border with the heads of the conspiracy.   A good many refugees had fled to England, and were to be seen in London "stately tragic figures, in proud threadbare cloaks," as Carlyle called them.   A cousin of Sterling's, Boyd by name, joined the band and perished in 1831, when the chief conspirators were arrested, by military execution, at Malaga.   The object of Tennyson's expedition is mysterious.   Probably the two friends expressed sympathy, learnt the designs of the rebellion, and returned to England to endeavour to excite public interest in the movement.

CHAPTER II

IN 1831 Tennyson left Cambridge, his father being ill and his presence at home being desired by his mother. A month later Dr. Tennyson died suddenly in his chair. This made a considerable difference in the fortunes of the family. Mrs. Tennyson was moderately well off; but the children were numerous and expensive. An arrangement, however, was made by which they leased the Rectory at Somersby from the new incumbent, and this arrangement remained in force till 1837. A great happiness resulted from Arthur Hallam's engagement to Emily Tennyson, and Hallam's visits to Somersby were eagerly expected ; he cheered them all with his bright unselfish spirit and "his gentle chivalrous manner."

Tennyson himself settled down to a quiet family life ; reading and writing much in solitude, and emerging from his seclusion to join the cheerful family group. He was devoted to his mother, treated her with delicate and dutiful attention, spending hours in reading to her in the voice "like the sound of a pinewood," as Carlyle said.   But he must have been an anxiety to his practical friends. He had published his first volume in 1830, and a second in the winter of 1832 (it is dated 1833) and now lived quietly his own life, without any attempt to enter a profession, dreaming his dreams, invested with the "inner central dignity" which was so characteristic of him, without obvious care for the future.   "I drag on somewhat heavily thro' the ruts of life" (he wrote to his aunt in 1833), "sometimes moping to myself like an owl in an ivy-bush . . . and sometimes smoking a pipe with a neighbouring parson and cursing O'Connell for as double-dyed a rascal as ever was dipped in the Styx of political villainy."   Sometimes he visited London and the "long unlovely street" where Hallam was reading law.   Sometimes he travelled with the latter, in England or on the continent, according to the condition of his finances.   Meanwhile he worked on, as Spedding said, "like a crocodile, sideways and onwards."

His health at this time had begun to cause him anxiety ; in 1831 he was haunted by the thought that he would lose his sight : "It would be a sad thing," he wrote, "to barter the universal light even for the power of 'Tiresias and Phineus, prophets old.'"   His appearance gave no hint of his state.   His eyes, as FitzGerald says, were dark, powerful, serene.   But the malady, whatever it

was, gave way before a simple diet.   It is evident
that much of his suffering was nervous and hypo-
chondriacal, and that his mode of life was probably
responsible.   He was fond of strong homely foods,
was probably careless of digestion and regular exercise, though always a great walker; he was also a
continuous smoker of strong tobacco.   Probably his
hours of solitude, the absence of stir and practical
activities and the monotonous tenor of his life had
to be paid for by hours of gloom.   Signs, too, of
definite nervous disturbance are not lacking.   He
suffered, it is known, from a curious mental obses-
sion, of the nature of catalepsy or incipient trance,
of which he himself gave in later years an accurate
account.   He called it, speaking to Tyndall, "a state
of transcendent wonder, associated with absolute
clearness of mind."   It seems to have been a
hypnotic state, more Oriental than Western in type,
induced by the repetition of some word, often his own
name, in which he seemed to lose his hold of external
things, and to float upon the tides of mystical contemplation,—"out of the body," as St. Paul says.

He might have sunk into settled invalidism, but
was preserved, partly by the influences of friendship,
partly by a settled scheme of work which he laid
down for himself,—reading ancient and modern
languages, history, philosophy and science,—partly
by his intense preoccupation in social movements,
or in the deeper politics which concern the welfare

of nations. He brooded much over the unsettled condition of the country, the misery of the poorer classes, the possible downfall of the Church and the confiscation of her property. A few letters of this period are preserved, rather elaborate and pompous in style, with a certain lofty humour penetrating them; his first volume had been reviewed in *Blackwood* in a patronising, boisterous article by Christopher North, which evoked from Tennyson the well-known lines on *Crusty Christopher* [1]; the tone of this poem is hardly consistent with that of a published letter, *posé* and apologetic, addressed privately to Wilson, deprecating further cudgelling. Perhaps it was with this and similar letters in his mind that he wrote :—

> Ye know that History is half-dream—ay even
> The man's life in the letters of the man.
> There lies the letter—but it is not he
> As he retires into himself and is :
> Sender and sent-to go to make up this,
> Their offspring of this union.

But by far the most interesting correspondence of the time, which would have given a true and intimate picture of his mind—the letters to Arthur Hallam—were destroyed after his friend's death by Hallam's father, the historian. The friendship between the two began at Cambridge. Tennyson had formed the highest hopes for Hallam's future. These kindred minds were deeply interested in the

[1] Published in the 1832 volume, and afterwards suppressed.

ardent problem of opening life. Together they had sounded the deeps of the spirit; the sensitive and overshadowed mind of Tennyson found in his friend a perfect and delicate sympathy, and an antidote to his natural gloom in the radiant gaiety and intense zest with which Hallam approached the mysteries of thought.

The dreadful blow fell in September, 1833. Arthur Hallam, staying at a hotel in Vienna with his father, to all appearances in perfect health, lay down on a sofa in the afternoon, and died in a few minutes from the rupture of some blood-vessel on the brain. A medical examination showed that he could not have lived long. He had inherited a fragile constitution, and the ceaseless strain of thought habitual to him told heavily upon him. It is strange that the disappointing portrait of him at Eton, taken a few years before, and representing a plump, rubicund, undistinguished young man, with an air of homely sense and virtue, gives no hint of delicacy and still less of genius. Moreover, what is still more strange, the existing literary remains of Arthur Hallam afford no explanation of what the individual peculiarity may have been which so dazzled his contemporaries. These writings can hardly be called more than promising.

The event plunged Tennyson into the deepest gloom; it was like losing part of himself. He became to himself, as Horace says, *Nec carus aeque*

nec superstes integer. He began, after the first shock
of grief was over, to write the immortal elegy, *In
Memoriam*, using a metre which had been used by
Ben Jonson and Lord Herbert of Cherbury, but of
which he believed himself to be the inventor, a simple
transposition of the common eight-syllabled quatrain.
He wrote without definite design, he says, and the
arrangement and combination of the elegies was an
afterthought.

The years flowed slowly on. In 1835 Tennyson
paid a visit to the Speddings at Mirehouse near
Bassenthwaite, the house of his friend's father.
The elder Mr. Spedding was a country gentleman
of a shrewd practical turn, a considerable mistrust
of poets and a remarkable faculty of minding his
own business. FitzGerald was there and made
very salient and interesting notes of the occasion.
Mr. Spedding the elder was, he says in a letter to
Mrs. Kemble written more than forty years later,
"a wise man who mounted his Cob after Breakfast
and was at his Farm till Dinner at two—then away
again till Tea, after which he sat reading by a shaded
lamp : saying very little, but always courteous, and
quite content with any company his Son might bring
to his house so long as they let him go his own way :
which indeed he would have gone whether they let
him or no. But he had seen enough of Poets not
to like them or their Trade : Shelley, for a time
living among the Lakes : Coleridge at Southey's

(whom perhaps he had a respect for—Southey I mean), and Wordsworth, whom I do not think he valued."

It was here that Tennyson read to FitzGerald late at night, in the silent house, fragments of poems which were to form the volumes of 1842, out of a little red book. Spedding also was permitted to read them aloud ; but Tennyson said he read too much as if there were bees about his mouth. Old Mr. Spedding used to object to his son spending so much time in this friendly criticism. "Well, Mr. FitzGerald," he used to say, "and what is it ? Mr. Tennyson reads, and Jim criticises ? Is that it ?" It was after this visit that FitzGerald wrote the memorable letter to his friend John Allen (23rd May, 1835) :—

"I will say no more of Tennyson than that the more I have seen of him, the more cause I have to think him great. His little humours and grumpinesses were so droll, that I was always laughing : and was often put in mind (strange to say) of my little unknown friend, Undine. I must, however, say, further, that I felt what Charles Lamb describes, a sense of depression at times from the overshadowing of a so much more lofty intellect than my own : this (though it may seem vain to say so) I never experienced before, though I have often been with much greater intellects : but I could not be mistaken in the universality of his mind. . . ."

Besides these characteristic notes there exist some
highly interesting pictorial sketches of the Bard ; one
is a back view, and shows his luxuriant locks; the
other, by Spedding, without technical excellence, but
of a convincing quality of fidelity, shows him seated
in an oak chair, wrapped in a cloak, with a book held
close to his face ; his feet are encased in slippers, and
one is thrust in front of the fire. The mouth is slightly
open, and there is a vague perplexity in the brow.

Spedding complained that at this time Tennyson
showed an " almost personal dislike of the present,
whatever it may be," and that he would not go to
Rydal though Wordsworth seemed inclined to welcome him there.   It was probably on this occasion
that the well-known contest took place between
FitzGerald and Tennyson as to who could produce
the ideally worst Wordsworthian line.   The result
was *A Mr. Wilkinson, a clergyman*, an achievement
to which both in later years laid claim.

In 1836 Tennyson's brother Charles married Miss
Louisa Sellwood; her elder sister, Emily, whom
Tennyson had seen before, acted as bridesmaid, and
it fell to Tennyson's lot to escort her to church.
Then it seems entered into his mind the hope
(which after a weary waiting was to be so singularly
blest) that he might win her for his wife.   At this
time it became necessary to leave Somersby.   The
family moved first to High Beech, in Epping Forest,
then a few years later to Tunbridge Wells; after

this to Boxley, near Maidstone, and finally to Cheltenham.

Belonging to this period is a characteristic correspondence with Monckton Milnes, which shows Tennyson at his best and liveliest. Milnes had extracted a promise from Tennyson to write in a Miscellany edited by the second Marquis of Northampton in aid of the family of a struggling literary man who had died without making provision for them. On his claiming the fulfilment of the promise, Tennyson declined, on the ground that he had supposed the request to be an "elegant fiction." Perhaps it rankled in his mind that he had lately been described, as FitzGerald told him, in a French review, as a young enthusiast of the graceful school of Tom Moore.

Tennyson went on to say that "to write for people with prefixes to their names is to milk he-goats; there is neither honour nor profit." He confesses that he has lately written a similar piece for a titled lady, but because she was beautiful. "But whether the Marquis be beautiful or not, I don't much mind; if he be, let him give God thanks and make no boast."

Milnes was very angry, and replied, it must be inferred, in an indignant and caustic tone. Whereupon Tennyson, in a letter of good-humoured bewilderment, gave way, and eventually sent to the Marquis the lyric *O that 'twere possible* which became the germ of *Maud.*

At this time Tennyson's position and prospects must have given considerable anxiety to his friends. He read, he smoked, he lounged, he worked at poetry, but he gave no signs of intending to publish, and seemed unlikely ever to make an independent position for himself. Wordsworth said, on reading *The Two Voices,* "He ought to have done greater things by this time." G. S. Venables wrote to press on him the advantages of living at Cambridge, evidently fearing that intellectual stagnation would ensue from his secluded life. "Do not continue to be so careless of fame and of influence." It is difficult not to gild the early and struggling years of great men with some of the dignity that seems so inseparable from their later life, and it is hard to imagine how unsatisfactory the position must have seemed to his friends. It really appeared as though a man of great genius and surpassing powers might drift into a hypochondriac and indolent life. But with majestic independence or dignified inertia Tennyson held on his way. He was often in London in these years, and though he did not go into general society, he saw much of his old friends; he was not a frequenter of clubs; but he liked rambling about, talking—we learn that he was famous for his powers of mimicry—dining in such seclusion as was attainable at quiet taverns, and accepting with good grace the visits of friends at his humble lodgings in the Strand. His tastes were simple enough. A perfect dinner was a beefsteak, a potato, a cut of cheese, a pint of port followed by a pipe; "all fine-natured men," he said, when bantered on his homely tastes in food, "know what is good to eat." He was interested, in a deep-minded abstruse way, in social movements and politics. He saw Carlyle, Rogers, Thackeray, Dickens, Landor, Leigh Hunt and Thomas Campbell, and came to be generally regarded as a man of high possibilities. Carlyle conceived a great admiration for him, though he spoke of him as a "life-guardsman spoilt by making poetry." Writing to Emerson, Carlyle described him as "a man solitary and sad, as certain men are, dwelling in an element of gloom, carrying a bit of Chaos about him, in short, which he is manufacturing into Cosmos . . . he preferred clubbing with his mother and some sisters, to live unpromoted and write Poems. . . . One of the finest-looking men in the world—a great shock of rough dusky dark hair; bright, laughing, hazel eyes; massive aquiline face, most massive yet most delicate; of sallow brown complexion, almost Indian looking; clothes cynically loose, free-and-easy, smokes infinite tobacco. His voice is musical, metallic, fit for loud laughter and piercing wail, and all that may lie between; speech and speculation free and plenteous; I do not meet in these late decades such company over a pipe! We shall see what he will grow to."

Again, to his brother John, Carlyle sent another word-portrait : "A fine, large-featured, dim-eyed, bronze-coloured, shaggy-headed man is Alfred ; dusky, smoky, free-and-easy ; who swims outwardly and inwardly, with great composure, in an articulate element as of tranquil chaos and tobacco-smoke ; great now and then when he does emerge ; a most restful, brotherly, solid-hearted man."

Carlyle thought and wrote scornfully as yet of Tennyson's poetry, and described him once as seated on a dunghill surrounded by dead dogs, which was his delicate way of alluding to the classical subjects at which Tennyson worked. When Tennyson charged him with this criticism Carlyle admitted with a grim smile that it was not a very lucid description.

The decade ending with Tennyson's marriage in 1850, when he was forty, was a fruitful period, rich in work, in experience, and in hope. In 1842 he published the two volumes which contained a selection of early poems, with a number of idylls and eclogues, simple pictures of English life. Tennyson felt with Wordsworth that upon the sacredness of home life depended the greatness and stability of a people. It was in this volume that he came home to the heart of the nation ; he passed from the exercise of pure imagination into the region of humanity, of domestic and national emotion. Whether this was an advantage from the purely poetic point of view may be debated ; but it is not possible to doubt that it widened and deepened his influence, and enabled him to appeal with remarkable force to a comprehensive circle. Even Carlyle, who thought lightly of all English poetry, said that in this book he "felt the pulse of a real man's heart . . . a right valiant, true, fighting, victorious heart."   Such poems as *The Gardener's Daughter, The Lord of Burleigh, Locksley Hall,* and the conclusion of *The May Queen,* touched the imagination and the emotion of a class of readers which *Ulysses, St. Agnes' Eve* and *Sir Galahad* would have left cold.

The new poems were mostly written in a foolscap parchment-bound account-book of blank paper, which went by the name of the " Butcher's Book." FitzGerald says, "The poems were written in A.T.'s very fine hand (he once said, not thinking of himself, that great men generally wrote 'terse' hands) towards one side of the large page ; the unoccupied edges and corners being often stript down for pipe lights, taking care to save the MS., as A. T. once seriously observed.   These pages . . . were one by one torn out for the printer, and, when returned with the proofs, were put in the fire."

Still, the destruction of these MSS. is a matter of comparatively little moment, as the poems were in most cases practically completed in his mind before being written down, the corrections after-

wards being very few; had he written rough drafts
and corrected them repeatedly in writing, then to
study the process of thought would have been
deeply interesting.

It is interesting to note the effect that the
volume of 1842 had upon Charles Dickens; he
wrote from Broadstairs in that year: "I have
been reading Tennyson all this morning on the
sea-shore. Among other trifling effects, the waters
have dried up as they did of old, and shown me all
the mermen and mermaids at the bottom of the
ocean; together with millions of queer creatures,
half fish and half fungus, looking down into all
manner of coral caves and seaweed conservatories;
and staring in with their great dull eyes at every
open nook and loophole." In this criticism is
finely exemplified the effect of pure suggestion
upon an imaginative mind.

It is difficult to give any connected record of the
incidents of these years; to begin with, they were
extremely uneventful; but there seems, too, to have
been an almost entire cessation of correspondence
between Tennyson and his friends. His mother
and sisters had settled at Tunbridge Wells, and the
Poet made his home with them; they then moved,
as I have said, to Boxley, near Maidstone; he was
often at Park House, in the neighbourhood, where
Edmund Lushington lived, who married Tennyson's
sister Cecilia. He went to London occasionally, and

C

indulged, when his funds permitted, in vague rambling tours. In 1845 he was at Eastbourne, hard at work on *The Princess*. The opening scene in the latter was drawn from a Mechanics' Institute fête held at Park House in 1842. *In Memoriam* had just been finished.

One disagreeable incident at this period proved fertile in misfortune for Tennyson; when the family were living at Beech Hill they had made the acquaintance of a certain Dr. Allen, an unpractical enthusiastic man, of an inventive turn, who had conceived the idea of wood-carving by machinery. His enthusiasm was infectious, and Tennyson sold some land which he possessed at Grasby in Lincolnshire, and invested the proceeds, together with all the other money he possessed, in the concern; he moreover persuaded his brothers and sisters to follow his example to a certain extent. The project collapsed, and the whole of Tennyson's independent income was gone; he had been hoping that he might soon, if things prospered, venture to marry, and now this seemed for ever impossible. The remorse at having lost the money of his brothers and sisters did not improve matters, and he was attacked with such severe hypochondria that for a time it was thought he could never recover. " I have drunk," he wrote, " one of those most bitter draughts out of the cup of life, which go near to make men hate the world they move in." Again he wrote:

" What with ruin in the distance and hypochondria
in the foreground, God help all ! "

The family now moved to Cheltenham, to a house
in St. James's Square; and Tennyson himself was
obliged to undergo a course of hydropathy under
which he slowly regained his health.

In 1845 he was offered and accepted a pension
of £200 a year from the Civil List. The intention
was communicated to him in a dignified letter from
Sir Robert Peel. It seems that the idea originated
with Carlyle, who insisted that Lord Houghton
should appeal for it; Lord Houghton appears to
have deprecated doing so, asking, " What will my
constituents say ? "

" Richard Milnes," said Carlyle, " on the Day of
Judgment, when the Lord asks you why you didn't
get that pension for Alfred Tennyson, it will not do
to lay the blame on your constituents; it is *you* that
will be damned."

Lord Houghton then went to Peel, who said that
there was a question whether Sheridan Knowles
should not rather receive a pension. Lord Houghton
decided the matter by inducing Peel to read
Ulysses.

Tennyson himself felt some qualms at accepting
it, as was only natural; but in the wreck of his
fortunes it no doubt helped to lift the burden.
Peel, moreover, had told him that he need not be
hampered by it in the public expression of any

opinion he might choose to take up. "So," wrote
Tennyson to his old friend and relative Rawnsley,
"if I take a pique against the Queen or the Court
or Peel himself, I may, if I will, bully them with as
much freedom, tho' not perhaps quite so gracefully
as if I were still unpensioned. Something in that
word 'pension' sticks in my gizzard; it is only the
name, and perhaps would 'smell sweeter' by some
other."

In 1846 he made a tour in Switzerland. "I was
satisfied," he wrote, "with the size of crags, but
mountains, great mountains disappointed me."

In the same year the fourth edition of the poems
came out, and Bulwer Lytton made a savage attack
upon him because of the pension, being under the
impression apparently that Tennyson belonged to a
wealthy family. Tennyson retorted in a poem of
concentrated bitterness, called *The New Timon
and the Poets*, in which Lytton is described as

<blockquote>The padded man that wears the stays.</blockquote>

This poem reveals in a high degree Tennyson's
power of personal invective, which as a rule he kept
severely in check. "Wretched work," he said long
afterwards, "*Odium literarium!* I never sent my
lines to *Punch*—John Forster did. They were too
bitter. I do not think that I should ever have
published them."

In 1847 *The Princess* appeared. Tennyson

never thought very highly of this graceful, light-hearted romance. The poem underwent considerable alterations, the six lyrical interludes being introduced in 1850, and in 1851 the "weird seizures" of the prince. These lyrics, such as *As Through the Land* and *Sweet and Low*, with the occasional poems introduced into the narrative, *Tears, idle tears* and the exquisite idyll *Come down O Maid from yonder mountain height*, belong to his very best work. He used to indicate certain passages in *The Princess* as among his best blank verse, notably the lines from the last canto :—

> Look up, and let thy nature strike on mine ;

but it is fair criticism to maintain that the simile which comes into this passage—

> In that fine air I tremble, all the past
> Melts mist-like into this bright hour, and this
> Is morn to more, and all the rich to-come
> Reels, *as the golden Autumn woodland reels*
> *Athwart the smoke of burning weeds*—

is too literary a simile, and is like a trench dug across the path of the simple and direct emotion which the speech reveals.

FitzGerald, like Carlyle, gave up all hopes of Tennyson after *The Princess*. He said that "none of the songs had the old champagne flavour," a criticism which somewhat vitiated the worth of the judgment. Moreover, it was noticed that nothing either by Thackeray or Tennyson met with FitzGerald's approbation unless he had seen it first in MS.

From 1846 to 1850 Tennyson lived mainly with his mother at Cheltenham, occupying a small disordered room at the top of the house, where papers lay in confusion on tables, chairs and floor, where he smoked innumerable pipes, and discoursed to an occasional friend who penetrated to his retreat on the deepest problems of life, mingling his talk with abundance of high-flavoured humour. He made a few friends at Cheltenham—Dobson, the Principal of the College, and Frederick Robertson, the "much-beloved" priest, of whom Tennyson said that the first time they met he himself could talk, from sheer nervousness, of nothing but *beer*, because he felt that Robertson admired his poems and wished "to pluck the heart from his mystery."

He was a great walker and took long rambles in the beautiful and secluded woodland country that lay about the little town. One interesting conversation is recorded. He was on a visit to London, and was found sitting with Thackeray, with a stack of shag tobacco, and a Homer, and the poems of Miss Barrett (Mrs. Browning) on the table. They praised her work, and Tennyson went on to speak of Catullus whom he called " the tenderest of Roman poets," quoting the delicious picture of the baby smiling at his father from his mother's breast, from the *Epithalamium.* Thackeray said, " I do not rate Catullus highly—I could do better myself." The next day Thackeray wrote a recantation penitently apologising for the "silly and conceited speech" he had made, saying, "At the time I thought I was making a perfectly simple and satisfactory observation." Tennyson's comment on this was, "No one but a noble-hearted man could have written such a letter."

Tennyson, when in London, used to take long walks at night with Carlyle, who would rave against the "jackasseries" of Government and the "acrid putrescence" of the suburbs. He used also to attend Rogers's breakfast parties, and had a sincere friendship for the self-conscious, tender-hearted old man, with his trick of bitter speech. "Peace be to him," Tennyson said long after, "often bitter but very kindly at heart. We have often talked of death together till I have seen the tears roll down his cheeks." Mrs. Carlyle gives a delightful picture of Tennyson at an evening party, where some private theatricals were performed, arranged by Dickens and Forster. "Passing through a long dim passage," she writes, "I came on a tall man leant to the wall, with his head touching the ceiling like a caryatid, to all appearance asleep, or resolutely trying it under the most unfavourable circumstances. 'Alfred Tennyson!' I exclaimed, in joyful surprise. 'Well!' said he, taking the hand I held out to him, and forgetting to let it go again. 'I did not know you were in town,' said I. 'I should like to know who you are,' said he, 'I know that I know you, but I cannot tell your name,'—and I had actually to name myself to him. Then he woke up in good earnest."

In 1848 he travelled in Cornwall. His journal is full of exquisite notes of scenery, conveyed in crisp jewelled phrases. It was here that he formed the resolution to take up the Arthurian legends seriously.

In May, 1850, *In Memoriam* was printed and given to a few friends; and shortly afterwards published anonymously. It seems impossible now that the authorship could have been doubted ; but one review spoke of it as "much shallow art spent on the tenderness shown to an Amaryllis of the Chancery Bar," and another critic pronounced that these touching lines evidently came "from the full heart of the widow of a military man."

But the volume was warmly welcomed by teachers such as Maurice and Robertson, who were still trying to harmonise the exact utterances of revelation with progressive science ; scientific men such as Tyndall, whose natural bias was strongly religious and emotional, were still more delighted to welcome one who showed that the spirit of science was alien neither to poetry nor religious emotion. Bishop Westcott felt on reading the poem that "the hope of man lay in the historic realisation of the gospel," and was deeply moved by the author's "splendid faith, in the face of the frankest acknowledgment of every difficulty, in the growing purpose of the sum of life, and in the noble destiny of the individual man."

CHAPTER III

THE year 1850 was indubitably the most memorable in Tennyson's life—the *annus mirabilis*. He reached the summit; and his life after that date was a peaceful, prosperous progress down the easy vale of days. He had come to the conclusion that his books seemed likely to produce, together with the pension and certain small property, a sufficient income for marriage. On the 13th of June, 1850, he married Emily Sarah Sellwood, sister of Mrs. Charles Tennyson-Turner, at Shiplake, near Henley. The bridegroom was forty, the bride a few years younger. It was the happiest and most fortunate act of a life that had hitherto been troubled and vexed; "the peace of God came into my life before the altar when I married her," he said.

Mrs. Tennyson was a woman of extraordinary loyalty and unfailing sweetness, with a delicate critical taste, cheerful, wise, courageous and sympathetic. She was an ideal companion for a great lonely nature in constant need of tender love and unobtrusive sympathy. It is the kind of marriage

(34)

that seems to make the institution deserve the name of a Sacrament. The rest of her life was entirely given to her husband. She sustained, encouraged and sheltered him ; though for many years she was an invalid and seldom left her sofa, yet the holy influence never diminished. It is worth quoting that a few weeks after the marriage Tennyson, sitting one evening smoking with Venables and Aubrey de Vere, said, between puffs of his pipe, as though pursuing a lonely train of thought, " I have known many women who were excellent, one in one way and one in another way, but this woman is the noblest I have ever known."

In the same year he was offered the Laureateship, vacant by the death of Wordsworth. The only other poet whose claims were seriously discussed was Rogers.

Tennyson wrote to Mr. H. D. Rawnsley, " I was advised by my friends not to decline it. . . . I have no passion for courts, but a great love of privacy."

After a short stay at Warninglid in Sussex, the Tennysons took up their abode in Twickenham, in a house called Chapel House, in Montpelier Row. It had a fine interior with some stately carving. Here the first years of a happy wedded life were spent. They travelled a good deal; but there are occasional glimpses of a beautiful home life, Tennyson reading aloud to his numerous callers in the little quiet garden. A child was born dead in 1851, but in 1852 Hallam, the present Lord Tennyson, was born. "Now I will tell you," he wrote to Forster, "of the birth of a little son this day. I have seen beautiful things in my life, but I have never seen anything more beautiful than the mother's face as she lay by the young child an hour or two after, or heard anything sweeter than the little lamblike bleat of the young one . . . he gave out a little note of satisfaction every now and then as he lay by his mother, which was the most pathetic sound in its helplessness I ever listened to." F. D. Maurice was asked to be sponsor and accepted the honour with tremulous responsibility. When Henry Hallam heard that the child was called Hallam he said with gruff amusement, "They would not name him Alfred lest he should turn out a fool, and so they named him Hallam."

In November, 1852, the Duke of Wellington died. The *Ode* was published on the morning of the funeral; but not quite in its present form. It was received, Tennyson said, with "all but universal depreciation . . . by the Press," though it is hard to see how its great qualities of simplicity and majesty came to be overlooked. Sometimes, it is true, the simplicity just overreaches itself:

> Thine island loves thee well, thou famous man,
> *The greatest sailor since our world began—*

is a hyperbole which is almost commonplace.

And now began the steady proffer of honours and
dignities which in England still testify, as a rule, to
a certain degree of eminence.   In 1853 he was
offered the Rectorship of the University of Edin-
burgh.   He replied gratefully, but saying that "he
could neither undertake to come to Edinboro', nor
to deliver an inaugural address at the time speci-
fied."   In 1855 came the offer of the Oxford
D.C.L., suggested by the present Archbishop of
Canterbury.   Tennyson accepted it and was received with immense enthusiasm, the shout of " In
Memoriam " from the undergraduates taking pre-
cedence of the cries for "Alma" and "Inkerman,"
with which Sir John Burgoyne and Sir de Lacy
Evans were greeted.

In 1853 he had visited Bonchurch with the idea
of taking a house there : he heard of Farringford,
visited it, approved of it, occupied and eventually
bought it.   It appears from a letter that he was
then making about £500 a year by his books, but
that his private means were otherwise scanty.   It
was a home for over forty years.

They had found Twickenham too accessible to
droppers-in, *obnoxia hospitibus.*   Yet the life on
which Tennyson was about to embark had its
dangers even for a man of his temperament.   His
love of solitary brooding, his morbidity, his self-
absorption, were all likely to be increased rather
than diminished by the new circumstances.   A

man without strongly defined agricultural tastes
or definite duties of a local or civic kind, is in
danger, in the country, of sinking into melancholy,
or if this is successfully resisted, and tranquillity
attained, of losing intellectual stimulus and mental
liveliness, of spinning round and round like a stick
caught in an eddy, away from the stream of things.

But it must be remembered that Tennyson's life
had hitherto been chiefly lived in backwaters, that
his nervous constitution was more adapted to bear
the strain of solitude, owing to his capacity for
absorption in a train of thought, for prolonged
brooding over great ideas, than to tolerate a life
frittered by ceaseless social invasions. He had,
moreover, his wife and children; he had his work,
which was continuous, if not daily; he was a diligent
and loving observer of nature—and, what must not
be forgotten—he had his fame, which enabled him
practically to command the society of any one he
desired at short notice : moreover Mrs. Tennyson
not only relieved him entirely of domestic burdens,
but kept them as completely hidden as though
they existed not—a triumph of grace of which
even the most devoted housewives are hardly
capable; she sheltered him, too, from worries
of an external kind, until her forces began to fail,
when her son slipped into her place with a noble
dutifulness as worthy of record as that of Æneas
himself.

The country life began at once with a deliberate resoluteness. The happy couple looked after their farm, visited the poor and sick of the village, swept up leaves, mowed grass, gravelled walks. Tennyson himself collected flowers, watched the ways of birds through spy-glasses, and took long walks with friends or the local geologist. All this was very wise and philosophical; perhaps he knew that these are just the simple pursuits which a man, if he once has the courage to embark upon them, finds opening out in all sorts of unexpected channels, and growing rather than diminishing in interest every year. He made companions, too, of his boys, and endeavoured to bring them up in simple and affectionate ways. It is interesting to note how careful Tennyson was to train the imaginative powers of his children. His son records how the younger boy Lionel was brought down from his bed one night, wrapt in a blanket, to see a comet; the child suddenly awaking and finding himself under the cool starry night, asked, "Am I dead?"

Into this quiet domestic life Tennyson sank, like a diving bird into a pool, with hardly a ripple. When Forster complained that his friends neither saw him nor heard from him, he replied that he never wrote letters except in answer, adding, "I beseech you and all my friends' most charitable interpretation of whatever I do or may be said to do."

In 1854 he was working hard at *Maud*, morning and evening ; his "sacred pipes," as he called them, were indulged in for half an hour after breakfast and half an hour after dinner, when no one was allowed to be with him, because he said that his best thoughts came to him then. His best working days he used to say were "in the early spring, when Nature begins to awaken from her winter sleep." He worked sitting in a hard high-backed wooden chair in his little room at the top of the house. As he sate or as he wrote he would murmur aloud his lines or fragments of lines : as some musicians compose with an instrument, while others never refer to one ; so some poets write and correct by eye, others by ear. Tennyson found that the spoken word helped him greatly, and that the constant reading aloud of his poems assisted him more than anything else to detect faults—a fact which illustrates the high value he set upon vowel sounds.

In the same year Millais came to stay with them. Tennyson made an interesting criticism, and as true as it is interesting, in conversation with the great painter, whose early splendid fault—if it can be called a fault—was a disproportionate insistence on the detail of a picture, a want of subordination of interest.

"If you have," said Tennyson, " human beings before a wall, the wall ought to be picturesquely painted, and in harmony with the idea pervading the picture, but must not be made obtrusive by the bricks being *too* minutely drawn, since it is the human beings that ought to have the real interest for us in a dramatic subject-picture." It is interesting that what Tennyson saw and expressed so clearly with reference to another art, he did not enough apply to his own : a poem like *The Princess* suffers from the very fault that he here so clearly indicates.

In 1855 came an incident which seems to have interested and encouraged Tennyson deeply, and to have made him feel that the poet after all could quicken the pulse of the working and fighting world. He was told that the English soldiers at the Crimea were many of them greatly excited about *The Charge of the Light Brigade,* and that they would like to have it in their hands. Tennyson had a thousand copies printed in slips and sent out; in this he restored the original version, retaining the phrase "someone had blundered," which was the germ of the poem, but which in accordance with criticism he had altered.

In 1855 his acquaintance with Robert Browning ripened into a true and loyal friendship. Mrs. Browning, writing to Mrs. Tennyson on the subject, said, on one occasion when Tennyson had been dining with them, that she had overheard in the next room, through the smoke, "some sentences" (of Tennyson's) "which in this materialistic low-talking world, it was comfort and triumph to hear

D

from the lips of such a man." She went on to try
and console Mrs. Tennyson for the harsh criticisms
that were appearing on *Maud*, which was published
in 1855. But the publication had one tangible
result; with the proceeds of the poem Tennyson
bought Farringford.

He now settled down to work at the *Idylls ;* the
subject had been in his mind for twenty years, and
in 1842 the *Morte d'Arthur* fragment had appeared.
He began with *Merlin and Vivien*, which he finished
in two months, and went on with *Geraint and Enid.*

It is interesting to note how the little touches of
everyday life were worked into the poem; he used
at the time to dig a good deal for exercise; one day
as he dug, a robin hopped round him, inspecting
his work in the hope of some rich grub being
thrown out;

As careful robins eye the delver's toil

was the result.

When the furniture from Twickenham was being
moved into Farringford and the house was in entire
confusion, the Prince Consort called, and made firm
friends with the Poet. Tennyson had met him
before only in a dream. The night before the
Laureateship was offered him he dreamed that the
Prince Consort had met him and kissed him. "Very
kind but very German," had been Tennyson's
thought.

There followed easy, prosperous years, with un-remitting, unhurried work, a quiet country life, diversified by visits from congenial friends, and plenty of leisurely travel both in England and abroad to stir the lazy pulses ; on these tours Tennyson's observation was much on the alert—many similes were briefly sketched in a few salient words for future use ; his observation seemed to have centred almost entirely on nature and natural objects ; there is little trace of any notes of humanity or human talk. He was still fretful at intervals over unintelligent critics whom he called "mosquitoes." In 1858 he delayed the publication of the newly written *Idylls*, and Jowett, who had a sincere mission for giving trenchant advice to his intimate friends if he saw them giving way to weaknesses, wrote a highly characteristic letter to remonstrate with him.

"Anyone," he wrote, "who cares about you is deeply annoyed that you are deterred by them ('mosquitoes') from writing or publishing. The feeling grows and brings in after years the still more painful and deeper feeling that they have prevented you from putting out half your powers. Nothing is so likely to lead to misrepresentation. Persons don't understand that sensitiveness is often combined with real manliness as well as great intellectual gifts, and they regard it as a sign of fear and weakness."

This is shrewd advice and faithfully given.

It was about this date that Mr. G. F. Watts's great picture of the Poet was painted, now in the possession of Lady Henry Somerset. It is the noblest and most ideal representation of the man. Out of the cloud of luxuriant hair towers the stately forehead, the eyes dim with a certain trouble of thought, but yet with an inward serenity ; the thin moustache and beard half hide, half accentuate the full strong lips. It is the face of a dreamer of immortal dreams.

In December, 1861, the Prince Consort died, and Tennyson wrote the *Dedication to the Idylls*, probably the simplest and most sincere complimentary poem ever penned. This led to his first interview with Queen Victoria. Tennyson said, "There was a kind of stately innocence about her." "I was conscious," he said, "of having spoken with considerable emotion to the Queen, but I have a very imperfect recollection of what I did say. Nor indeed . . . do I very well recollect what Her Majesty said to me ; but I loved the voice that spoke, for being very blind I am much led by the voice, and blind as I am and as I told her I was, I yet could dimly perceive so great an expression of sweetness in her countenance as made me wroth with those imperfect *cartes de visite*. . . ."

From this interview dated a sincere friendship between the Queen and her Laureate. In 1863 the Queen asked him what she could do for him, no doubt with the idea of conferring some dignity upon him. Tennyson's reply was, "Nothing, Madam, but shake my two boys by the hand. It may keep them loyal in the troublous times to come."

At this time he was much taken up with his experiments in classical metres; *Boädicea* was the one of which he was most proud; but he realised the extreme difficulty of finding suitable words in sufficient numbers to finish the lines with.

Indeed the metre of *Boädicea* has only a very superficial resemblance to the metre of the *Attis* of Catullus[1] which he imitated. Tennyson's metre is in reality only a trochaic, with dactylic substitutions in certain feet; but this matters little, and the poem is a magnificent cataract of rhythmical sound.

A good instance of Tennyson's superficial roughness is given in a reminiscence of this period. Mr. Thomas Wilson was staying at Farringford and saw much of the Tennysons. He was suffering from fits of deep melancholy; on one of these occasions he made some complaint to Tennyson hinting at a desire for death. Tennyson replied, with genial gruffness, "Just go grimly on!"—and on another occasion, "If you wish to kill yourself, don't do it here; go to Yarmouth and do it decently." Mr. Allingham, who was there at the same time, said that he talked

---

[1] A nonsense line in the metre of Catullus would run :—

Fŏr ŭbōut | thĕ spāce | ŏf sīx | yeãrs ĭt ŭppēared | ĭnĭmĭtăblĕ.

to Tennyson about Browning. "I can't understand
how he should care for my poetry," said Tennyson.
"His new poem has fifteen thousand lines. There's
copiousness for you! Good-night!"

As years went on life became, so to speak, less
and less eventful. One of the chief interests of Farringford was the endless succession of distinguished
guests that came there. Tennyson's hours of work
were strictly respected, but it seems as though when
there were friends in the house he had little leisure
for solitary work. He still took a short time after
breakfast and a short time after dinner by himself;
but he walked with his guests in the morning, sate
to talk with them in the afternoon and evening.
His abundant geniality and sociability when he was
in the presence of those who understood him was
in curious contrast to his almost abnormal shyness,
his hatred for what he called "the humbug of
Society." He often made friends, particularly with
people of simplicity of character, with extraordinary
rapidity; and his true hospitality was shown in his
accustomed farewell, "Come whenever you can."

For instance, in 1864 Garibaldi came to see him,
and planted a tree at Farringford; the two great men
repeated Italian poetry together. "Are you a poet?"
Tennyson said to him. "Yes," said the warrior.
They talked together; Tennyson said, "I doubt
whether he understood me perfectly, and his meaning was often obscure to me." Tennyson advised

him not to talk politics in England. After he was gone Tennyson praised the majestic simplicity of his manners and said that in worldly matters he seemed to have the "divine stupidity of a hero."

The same year he made an expedition to Brittany, with the intention of visiting places traditionally connected with the Arthurian legend. Tennyson of course located his Camelot in "a land of old up-heaven from the abyss." This was imagined to lie to the west of Land's End, and the Scilly Isles to be the tops of its submerged mountains.

In 1864 the *Enoch Arden* volume was published, probably the most popular of all Tennyson's works. Sixty thousand copies were sold in a very short time. The poem of *Enoch Arden* itself was written in a fortnight in a little summer-house at Farring-ford. In 1865 he visited Waterloo, and Weimar. He went to Goethe's houses, and found the sight of Goethe's old boots and bottles interesting and pathetic. In October, 1865, he was at work at the new poem of *Lucretius*.

In the following year he sent his boy to Marl-borough, where his old friend Bradley was head-master. An interesting account of his visit is preserved. He told many stories and read aloud obediently. After dinner one night he was asked by Mrs. Bradley to read *The Grandmother*; he refused, saying, "I can't read *The Grandmother* properly except after breakfast when I am weak and tremulous; fortified by dinner and a glass of port I am too vigorous." He then read *The Northern Farmer* and at the conclusion turned to a Belgian governess who was present and asked her how much she understood. "Pas un mot, Monsieur!" He went on reading, laughing, as he read, until the tears came, and carefully explaining the points to the governess. This gives a pleasing picture of his simple kindliness.

He subscribed at this time to the testimonial to Governor Eyre, whose excessive severity in Jamaica had caused great indignation. This act of Tennyson's was severely commented upon. His own view was that Governor Eyre had nipped in the bud an outbreak that might have equalled the Indian Mutiny in horror.

In 1867 it was thought that Mrs. Tennyson required some bracing change from the soft air of Farringford; and Tennyson himself began to suffer from the curiosity and impertinence of summer pilgrims to Farringford. Accordingly he bought a secluded tract of ground near Haslemere, on the headland called Blackdown, which stood high and commanded a magnificent view of the southern plains : he named it Aldworth, from a village with which his family had been connected; and Mr. Knowles, now editor of the *Nineteenth Century*, then practising as an architect, built a house there from the Poet's rough design. The house is stately, and the details are beautiful—but it lacks charm.

He was invited in December, 1867, by W. H. Thompson, Master of Trinity, to stay with him at Cambridge, and replied in a delightfully character-istic note :—

"A smoking-room! If I put pipe to mouth *there*, should I not see gray Elohim ascending out of the earth, him whom we capped among the walks in golden youth, and hear a voice, 'Why hast thou disquieted me to bring me up?' I happened to say to Clark that, from old far-away undergraduate recollections of the unapproachable and august se-clusion of Trinity Lodge, Cambridge, I should feel more blown out with glory by spending a night under your roof, than by having lived Sultan-like for a week in Buckingham Palace. Now, you see, I was not proposing a visit to you, but speaking as after wine and over a pipe, and falling into a trance with my eyes open."

In the following year, 1868, he was working at Hebrew ; the foundation-stone of Aldworth was laid on the 23rd of April, Shakespeare's birthday. In the following month *Lucretius* was published in *Macmillan's Magazine*, which drew a characteristic note from Jowett to Mrs. Tennyson :—

"I thought *Lucretius* a most noble poem, and that is the universal impression. I cannot see any reason why Alfred should not write better and better as long as he lives, and as Mr. Browning says that he hopes and intends to do. I know that a poet is an inspired person, who is not to be judged by ordinary rules, nor do I mean to interfere with him. But I can never see why some of the dreams of his youth should not still be realised "—the last sentence probably refers to the contemplated completion of the *Idylls*.

In September of the same year he began *The Holy Grail* and finished it in about a week, "like a breath of inspiration." He sent a proof to Mr. Palgrave, who wrote that he had ventured to show it to Max Müller. Tennyson replied :—

"You distress me when you tell me that, without leave given by me, you showed my poem to Max Müller : not that I care about Max Müller's seeing it, but I do care for your not considering it a sacred deposit. Pray do so in future ; otherwise I shall see some boy in some Magazine making a lame imitation of it, which a clever boy could do in twenty minutes—and though his work would be worth nothing, it would take away the bloom and freshness from mine. . . .

"Please attend to my request about *The Grail* and *The Lover's Tale*, and show them to no one, or if you can't depend upon yourself, forward them to me."

In 1869 his old College of Trinity, Cambridge, elected him an "Honorary Fellow," a distinction he greatly valued.

In 1872 he was working at *Gareth and Lynette;*
he wrote to Mr. Knowles that he "found it more
difficult to deal with than anything except perhaps
Aylmer's Field." With the publication of that
idyll he thought the cycle complete; but later on,
feeling that some introduction to *Merlin and
Vivien* was necessary, he wrote *Balin and Balan.*

CHAPTER IV

IN 1873 Mr. Gladstone offered the Poet a baronetcy from the Queen. Tennyson replied that he and Mrs. Tennyson did not desire it for themselves, but would wish it to be assumed by his son at any age it might be thought right to fix upon. He added that he expected that this was outside all precedent, and said that he hoped there was not the least chance of the Queen's construing it into a slight of the proffered honour. "I hope," he added, "that I have too much of the old-world loyalty left in me not to wear my lady's favours against all comers, should you think that it would be more agreeable to Her Majesty that I should do so." Mr. Gladstone replied that it would be an innovation to confer an honour on a son in a father's lifetime; and Tennyson thereupon declined the honour altogether with obvious relief.

His friendship with Mr. Gladstone grew and deepened. In 1874, at the time of the Dissolution, Tennyson wrote: "Care not, you have done great work, and if even now you rested, your name would be read in one of the fairest pages of English history." He went on to add that in some points of policy they had differed; as years went on they differed still more widely. When Mr. Gladstone took up the cause of Irish Home Rule, Tennyson wrote, in reply to a question on the subject, " I love Mr. Gladstone, but I hate his present policy."

In 1874 Mrs. Tennyson became seriously ill, and was for the rest of her life, over twenty years, practically confined to her sofa. She was, according to Jowett, " one of the most beautiful, the purest, the most innocent, the most disinterested persons whom I have ever known." He went on to say that "it is no wonder that people speak of her with bated breath, as a person whom no one would ever think of criticising, whom every one would recognise, in goodness and saintliness, as the most *unlike* any one whom they have ever met."

Jowett went on to say that she was probably her husband's best critic; certainly the one whose authority he would most willingly have recognised. He spoke of her saintliness, which had nothing puritanical about it, her humour, her considerateness, her courage. She preserved not only life but youth under invalid conditions; and combined with great capacity for domestic management an extraordinary interest in religious, political and social movements, with an unflinching faith, and an eye firmly directed to what was beautiful and great.

Many friends of the family seem to have deliberately held that Mrs. Tennyson was as great as her
husband ; Jowett adds that had such a criticism
been repeated to her, she would merely have
wondered that any one could seriously have supposed
that there was any comparison possible. It must
be reckoned among the many and great felicities of
Tennyson's life, the felicities which seem to have
been so deliberately bestowed upon him, that the
presence and influence of such a wife was given him
till his latest day. Probably even he himself, intensely and continuously grateful as he was to her,
hardly realised how much she did for him in the
way of open sympathy and still more of deft and
uncomplaining management of somewhat difficult
and intricate household conditions.

> Dear, near and true, no truer Time himself
> Can prove you, tho' he make you evermore
> Dearer and nearer.

In 1874 Mr. Disraeli offered Tennyson a baronetcy
from the Queen, for the second time, in a character-
istically pompous letter, beginning, "A Government
should recognise intellect. It elevates and sustains
the spirit of a nation." He went on to say that
the Queen had shown her sympathy with science,
but that it was more difficult to recognise the
claims of literature because "the test of merit
cannot be so precise."

Tennyson replied as he had done to Gladstone,

refusing the honour for himself, and asking that it
might be conferred on his son after death.   Mr.
Disraeli replied that this was contrary to precedent,
and Tennyson again acquiesced.

As a rule he was very unwilling to join any
society or club that might make claims on his
time or require his attendance.   I imagine that a
definite engagement always hung heavy on the
spirits of the Poet.   But he made an exception in
favour of a remarkable society, called the Metaphysical Society, the inception of which was due to
Mr. Knowles.

The intention of the society was to discuss the
question of Christian Evidences with entire frankness, and to associate with pronounced Anglicans
men of every other shade of religious thought, such
as Roman Catholics, Unitarians, Nonconformists
and even Agnostics.   The lists of the society included almost all the advanced thinkers of the day,
politicians, scientists, philosophers and literary men.
It lasted for over ten years, and Tennyson even
consented, once at least, to preside.   The result of
the discussions was never made public, but Lord
Tennyson says that his father was more profoundly
convinced than ever by them of "the irrationality
of pure materialism," and thought that the theo-
logians of the present day were much more enlightened than their predecessors.

The society came to an end in 1880, Huxley

asserting that it died of "too much love." Tennyson
himself said humorously that it perished because
after ten years of strenuous effort no one had succeeded in even defining the term "Metaphysics."
It seems that practically Tennyson took no part in
the discussions.

Tennyson's mind was now actively turning to
the drama, and this will perhaps be the best
place to discuss briefly the literary merits of the
plays. He published *Queen Mary* in 1875, which
formed with *Harold* and *Becket* what he called
his historical trilogy.

The plays had a political or rather a national
motif. They were intended to portray "the
making of England." In *Queen Mary* he aimed
at representing the establishment of religious
liberty for the individual, in *Becket* the struggle
between the Crown and the Church, in *Harold*
the conflict of the three rival races, Danes, Saxons
and Normans for supremacy, and the "forecast of
the greatness of our composite race." It is to be
noted how large a part the religious element plays

in all the three. In *The Foresters* he tried to sketch
the state of the people during the period of the
Magna Carta, when the triumph of political liberty
over Absolutism began.

He had always taken a profound interest in the
drama, and it is interesting to note how the subjects were carefully chosen to fill gaps in the

sequence of Shakespeare's historical or chronicle plays. The drama was very much in his thoughts; he believed in it as a great humanising and elevating influence; he thought that when education should have raised the literary standard of the people, the stage would be of enormous influence. He even went so far as to hope that educational and municipal bodies would take to producing plays so as to form part of an Englishman's education, in the same way that the drama formed a part of the ordinary life of the Greeks at the period of their highest greatness.

He had a strong belief, moreover, in his own dramatic power; he liked the analysis of human motive and character. He was an enthusiastic critic of the drama, and entered with interest into the minutest details of scenic effect. His aim was to produce plays of high poetic excellence, and to put them into the hands of competent managers and actors for stage production. He was encouraged to persevere in the task by such authorities as Spedding, George Eliot and G. H. Lewes, and was on the whole satisfied with the results. It must be remembered that he was sixty-five when he began this venture.

The result, however, from the point of view of literature is, except perhaps in the case of *Harold*, even lamentable. It was as though a musician who had reached almost perfection on the violin,

E

took up at threescore the practice of the organ.
He was at an age when his mind was fully stored
with poetical substance ; the melody of his instrument was entirely under his control, his brain was
furnished with exquisite observation, and fertile
with simple emotions. Moreover, owing to his
great vitality, he had not yet outlived his power
of sympathy with youth, and he still retained
an abundance of that wondering joy in nature
and life with which things or thoughts of beauty
come home to the apprehension of the child,
and which is of the essence of all lyrical
poetry.

All this was sacrificed. He undertook instead
the practice of an art with which he was not
familiar, the painting in brief and characteristic
touches complex characters in a crowded canvas.
It is melancholy that no friend was found to tell
him that dramatic situations were precisely those in
which he had invariably failed, though it might have
proved a congenial task for Jowett. In monologue,
without the disturbing play of other influences, he
had done wonders ; his mind was of the brooding
kind that could throw itself intensely and profoundly
into a single character. Again and again he had
shown this, not only in his serious poems, but in
the humorous rustical figures whose very heart he
had laid open. He could even in a stately Hellenic
fashion contrive a slow duologue between two per-

sons whose characters he had fully penetrated. Yet even here he had produced an effect of stiffness and solemnity. But his mind was quite without the vivacity and the minuteness which can throw itself with instinctive rapidity into the swift give-and-take of dramatic situation ; he was no *desultor,* as the Romans said.

The consequence is that the plays, though the execution is faultless, somehow lack interest ; the wood is laid in order, but the fire does not kindle. It is very difficult to say why they do not arouse emotion, but the tragedy and the pathos have no transporting power. They leave the heart cold. In Shakespeare, with a far simpler outfit, a sudden spring seems to be touched, and we are in a new world. But it is possible to read Tennyson's plays wondering why no emotion is awakened. The reader feels all the time that it is like Tennyson's description of Maud's face —

> Faultily faultless, icily regular, splendidly null,
> Dead perfection, no more.

It is remarkable that such letters as are given in the *Life* praising his plays are as a rule from historians.

J. A. Froude wrote :—

" You have reclaimed one more section of English history from the wilderness and given it a form in which it will be fixed for ever. No one since

Shakespeare has done that. . . . You have given us the greatest of all your works."

About *Becket* Mr. Bryce wrote :—

"There is not, it seems to me, anything in modern poetry which helps us to realise as your drama does, the sort of power the Church exerted on her ministers."

Robert Browning, it is true, was still more laudatory, writing about *Queen Mary* :—

"Conception, execution, the whole and the parts, I see nowhere the shade of a fault, thank you once again!"

But the view taken of *Queen Mary* was not wholly favourable. Coventry Patmore wrote to a friend :—

"I will let you have Tennyson's play shortly. It is better than I expected—for it is not *weak*. But it is quite uninteresting. Every character is repulsive, and the sentimental themes, Mary's love for Philip and disappointment at not bringing him an heir, wholly unattractive. The moral is no better, simply the 'No Popery' cry—the straw at which Lord John Russell's, Gladstone's and so many other drowning reputations have clutched in vain. I fancy it will not serve the Laureate's purpose any better than it has served Mr. Gladstone's. Surely there is no passion which, when indulged, becomes so strong and vile as the love of popularity."

And again, after attending a performance, he wrote :—

"I never saw any play nearly so dismal or in-effective as *Queen Mary*. Though it has only been out a week or two, the theatre was three parts empty, and what audience there was seemed to be of the most snuffy kind. So deadly stupid were they, that when Mary said, 'We are Queen of England, Sir, not Roman Emperor,' they did not catch the grossly obvious applicability of the sentence to what is now going on, until I began to clap and beat the floor with my stick ; then it dawned upon a few ; and at last about half the poor people caught the idea and clapped too ; and a gentleman behind me said to his ladies, 'That's because of the Royal Titles Bill.' I thought of Dr. Vaughan's experience—after going about the whole world—that the English ranked in stupidity next to the negroes."

Everything was done that could be done by en-thusiastic and capable stage management. The plays, especially *Becket*, enjoyed a moderate success, a convincing proof of how deep and widespread was the affection and admiration with which Tenny-son was regarded by the public. "Fame is love disguised !"

CHAPTER V

I N 1878 the Poet's second son, Lionel, was married
to the daughter of Frederick Locker-Lampson,
and for several years about this time Tennyson took
a house in London from February to Easter "to rub
our country rust off," and to be near his son. Here
he saw on easy terms many of the great men of the
time ; and as showing how active his interest in
practical politics was, a reminiscence of a visit to
the veteran Earl Russell at Pembroke Lodge is
valuable. They shook hands over the necessity of
continuity in foreign policy.

Many visits were paid by Tennyson, when he was
in London, to Carlyle. The last words recorded as
having passed between them are touching. Tennyson had said that he would like to get away from
all the turmoil of civilisation and go to a tropical
island.

"Oh ay," said Carlyle, who was sitting in his
dressing-gown, "so would I, to India or somewhere.
But the scraggiest bit of heath in Scotland is more
to me than all the forests of Brazil. I am just

twinkling away, and I wish I had had my Dimittis long ago."

In 1879 Tennyson's brother, Charles Tennyson-Turner, died. There had always been a great affection between the two, and Alfred often spent part of the summer at his brother's Lincolnshire vicarage; that Mrs. Tennyson-Turner and Mrs. A. Tennyson were sisters drew the bond still closer.

The Laureate had a great admiration for his brother's sonnets, to a volume of which, published in 1880, he contributed some prefatory verses; it is interesting to note that almost the only form of poetical writing that Alfred Tennyson did not to any great extent attempt was the sonnet; and the sonnets he wrote are written in a half-hearted way and do not rank among his best work. There is little doubt that the recognition of his brother's superior skill in sonnet-writing deterred him from that form of composition; just as Charles himself confessed that Alfred's lyric skill made him feel for some years that it was hopeless to attempt to write poetry, from no petty jealousy, but from the discouragement which in sensitive minds attends on the contemplation of superior skill.

The bereavement made Alfred Tennyson very unwell, and he was afflicted by the hallucination of hearing perpetual ghostly voices. Sir Andrew Clark, who had become his doctor, ordered change, and Venice laid the ghosts.

It was on this tour that Tennyson made his *Frater
Ave*, a poem in which the theme is not developed,
which has no particular thought struck out, and
contains but one felicitous descriptive epithet, of
the twin-fruited kind that he loved—but which
remains one of the most perfect and purest pieces
of vowel music in the language, like a low sweet
organ-prelude, a snatch of magical sound.

In 1880, in his seventy-first year, he published a
volume of Poems and Ballads, which contains little
of permanent value except *The Revenge*. This
volume illustrates in a striking manner the decay
of his poetical faculty. In the earlier poems it is
noticeable how sweet, simple and even commonplace were the themes that aroused his emotion;
tender idyllic subjects of love and life were his
favourite inspirations, and even where the motive is
tragical all violent action is instinctively avoided,
and the scene is given through the haze of prospect or retrospect. He worked in the spirit of the
Horatian maxim—*Ne coram populo pueros Medea
trucidet*—or else pictorially and luxuriantly, with
abundant dwelling upon the details of the picture,
as in *The Lady of Shalott*. As he got older he
seemed to require more definite, strong, dramatic
situations, of horror or tragedy, or poignant emotion, to stir the slower current of his blood. Such
a poem as *Rizpah*, though it may be admired as
powerful, depends quite as much upon the forceful-

ness of the matter as upon the beauty of manner.
The Children's Hospital is another of the same class
—touching in its intention, but yielding to unworthy
prejudice, and not exhibiting the magical quality.
The Cup and *The Falcon* were also completed,
melancholy monuments.

All this time we have pleasant touches of the
serene home-life. William Allingham, who was staying with him, told him that Dr. Martineau at the
age of seventy-five had just climbed a mountain
4,000 feet high. Tennyson's answer is characteristic of the simple vanity which so often appeared
in his talk. "When I was sixty-seven I climbed a
mountain 7,000 feet high: the guide said he never
saw a man of my age *si léger.*"

In 1881 he sate to Millais for the portrait, which
the artist said was the finest he ever painted, belonging to Mr. Knowles. In November, 1882, the
unlucky play, *The Promise of May,* was produced.
It was supposed to be an attack on Free Thought
and Socialism, and attracted considerable attention
from the fact that the late Marquis of Queensberry
rose in his place in the middle of one of the performances and protested in the name of Free-thinkers
against "Mr. Tennyson's abominable caricature."
It seems to the ordinary reader a piece of sentimental melodrama, but Tennyson wrote of the play
that he had striven to bring the true drama of
character and life back again. "I gave them one

leaf out of the great book of truth and nature."
The idealist may humbly hope that similar leaves
are comparatively rare.

In these days he often stayed at the Deanery,
Westminster, with his old friends the Bradleys,
where he felt entirely at home. One day he
wandered about the Abbey and climbed up into a
chantry during service, which sounded sweetly
along the aisles. Tennyson said to his son, " It
is beautiful—but what empty and awful mockery if
there were no God."

In 1883 he had a long interview with the Queen
and talked quietly of death and immortality. The
close of the interview may be given in the Queen's
own simple words :—

" When I took leave of him, I thanked him for his
kindness, and said I needed it, for I had gone
through much, and he said, ' You are so alone on
that terrible height ; it is terrible. I've only a
year or two to live, but I shall be happy to do anything for you I can—send for me whenever you
like.' I thanked him warmly."

" He was very kind," was the Queen's touching
impression of his attitude towards her.

In September, 1883, he went a cruise with Sir
Donald Currie on the *Pembroke Castle*. Mr. Gladstone was of the party. At Kirkwall Tennyson
and Mr. Gladstone received the freedom of the
burgh, and Mr. Gladstone returned thanks for both

in a speech of graceful humility. The conversation between the two seems to have been interesting and to have brought out the fact that Gladstone talked as a rhetorician, with complicated analogies and with exquisitely complete parentheses, while Tennyson was incisive, brief and pointed. At Copenhagen a distinguished party came on board to luncheon. The Kings of Denmark and Greece with their Queens, and the Czar and Czarina. Tennyson read a couple of poems by request, and when the Czarina complimented him, he took her for a Maid of Honour, patted her on the shoulder, and said, "Thank you, my dear!"

It was on the *Pembroke Castle* that Mr. Gladstone offered Tennyson a peerage. His view was that a baronetcy, which in Sir Walter Scott's days represented the respectful homage of a Government for literature, was inadequate; he went on to say that he believed greatly in Tennyson's political wisdom.

It is amusing that Mr. Gladstone should have said gravely to Hallam Tennyson that he had one fear—that the Poet might insist on wearing his wide-awake in the House of Lords.

Tennyson himself was not very much in favour of accepting the peerage, but he undoubtedly had a great and increasing interest in national politics, and was not averse to taking a hand in them in a dignified way; he was also anxious that his son should eventually have a chance of playing a part in the political world—and he was, moreover, quite sensible of the fact that it meant a high recognition of the practical power of literature. "Why should I be selfish," he wrote to a friend, "and not suffer an honour . . . to be done to literature in my name?" He therefore reluctantly consented. "By Gladstone's advice," he said, "I have consented to take the peerage, but for my own part I shall regret my simple name all my life."

He took his seat in March, 1884, and sate on the cross-benches. He gave a vote for the Extension of the Franchise in July, 1884, but his attendances were very few, though it is evident from the records that the incident stirred his active interest in politics very greatly. He wrote several dignified and sensible letters on points mostly connected with the Franchise; and he was interested in the question of Disestablishment, and measures affecting agriculture.

In 1885 was published *Tiresias and other poems*: it contained an idyll *Balin and Balan*, which was written soon after *Gareth and Lynette*, a painful and tragic story, and not of marked technical excellence.

The Ancient Sage, a very personal and autobiographical poem, is perhaps the most interesting of the poems—but mainly from a biographical point of view. Here also were included the musical lines, *To Virgil*, which are on the old level.

In 1886 a great grief fell on him; his son Lionel, a young man of high promise, great unselfishness and vigour of character, with both literary and administrative ability, died, while returning from India, from fever, and was buried at sea. Tennyson was in his seventy-seventh year and felt the blow more acutely than is common with the old.

"The thought of Lionel's death tears me to pieces," he said, "he was so full of promise and so young." Tennyson was working at the sequel to *Locksley Hall*, and though the poem will be considered separately, it may be said that the reflex of his melancholy mood is only too plainly visible throughout.

The disabilities of age came gently upon him; he was often obliged to drive instead of walking, but his observation, in spite of failing eyesight, his sense of beauty and his interest in homely things continued wonderfully strong.

It is painful to see to what an extent, in these later years, he was overshadowed by pessimism. The faith in development, in the huge design of God which is so nobly defined in *In Memoriam*, seems to have to a great extent deserted him. The signs of the times alarmed and disquieted him. He felt as if the nation were on the brink of a great catastrophe. "You must not be surprised at anything that comes to pass in the next fifty years," he said, "all ages are ages of transition, but this is an awful moment of transition. It seems to me as if there were much less of the old reverence and chivalrous feeling in the world than there used to be."

Again he said solemnly, "When I see Society vicious and the poor starving in great cities, I feel that it is a mighty wave of evil passing over the world."

This last is an essentially unreal utterance—it is the " fear of that which is high"—the shadow of age, when the grasshopper becomes a burden. Tennyson had no means of knowing whether Society was vicious or not ; less indeed than when he was young, because he lived so entirely remote from it ; and as to the starving of the poor in great cities, there can be little doubt that the condition of the poor had altered only for the better since the Poet's youth. These broodings are mainly the depressed reveries of age, which cannot throw off melancholy reflection. Tennyson lacked the enduring optimism so characteristic of Robert Browning. Still, in spite of his pessimistic fear of widespread corruption and impending revolution, there was much that was tender, reverent and hopeful in his talk. "The better heart of me beats stronger at seventy-four than ever it did at eighteen," he once said.

There was much wisdom too in many of his

sociological talks: speaking of the sense of unity
in Society he used to acknowledge that it had
greatly increased since his own youth.

"The whole of Society," he said, "is at present
too like a jelly; when it is touched it shakes from
base to summit. As yet the unity is of weakness
rather than of strength. . . . Our aim therefore
ought to be not to merge the individual in the
community, but to strengthen the social life of the
community, and foster the individuality."

In 1888 he had a serious illness—rheumatic gout
brought on by walking in rain and getting drenched.
For a time he was very ill, and bore his illness with
great patience and even cheerfulness, making an
epigram when he was at his worst about the pain
killing the devil born in him eighty years before.
To his doctors he talked politics and said many
practical and sensible things, such as, "Every
agitator should be made to prove his means of
livelihood." For a time his life was despaired of;
when he was lying thus, Jowett wrote Lady Tennyson a fine letter, evidently intended to be read to
the Poet :—

". . . Give my love to him and tell him that I
hope he is at rest, knowing that we are all in the
hands of God. I would have him think sometimes
that no one has done more for mankind in our own
time, having found expression for their noblest
thoughts and having never written a line that he

would wish to blot; and that this benefit which he has conferred on the English language and people will be an everlasting possession to them, as great as any poet has ever given to any nation, and that those who have been his friends will always think of him with love and admiration, and speak to others of the honour of having known him. He who has such record of life should have the comfort of it in the late years of it: there may be some things which he blames, and some which he laments, but as a whole he has led a true and noble life, and he need not trouble himself about small matters. He may be thankful for the great gift which he has received, and that he can return an account of it. It seems to me that he may naturally dwell on such thoughts at this time, although also, like a Christian, feeling that he is an unprofitable servant, and that he trusts only in the mercy of God."

This letter is written in a high and noble vein, like the consolations of an ancient philosopher touched by a larger hope,—although the self-satisfaction which it recommends is perhaps more natural for others to read into the thoughts of a great man than for the great man to indulge in himself.

In April Sir Andrew Clark came to see him, in spite of the fact that he had been summoned to see the Shah. Sir Andrew had replied that he could not obey his Majesty as he had promised to visit his friend the old Poet. The Shah received this refusal very graciously and sent Sir Andrew a Persian Order.

Sir Andrew said that though Tennyson had been as near death as a man could be without dying, he was perfectly healthy and sound, adding that "he could not see where the door would open for his exit from life."

After his recovery he went for a cruise in the *Sunbeam*, lent him by Lord Brassey; he was in high spirits and told many stories. Aubrey de Vere was mentioned, and Tennyson said that Aubrey de Vere's idea of eternal punishment would be to listen to Huxley and Tyndall disputing eternally on the non-existence of God.

On his eightieth birthday many letters of admiration and love came to him. After reading one he said, "I don't know what I have done to make people feel like that towards me, except that I have always kept my faith in Immortality."

In December, 1889, appeared *Demeter and other poems*; these were wonderful productions for a man of his age, though not particularly memorable in themselves.

In October, 1889, he had written *Crossing the Bar* on a day when he went from Aldworth to Farringford; he made it in his mind, and wrote it out after dinner. It is traditionally related that the poem was read aloud to an old servant, a nurse, who had asked him "to write a hymn". On hearing it read,

F

she burst into tears and said, "It isn't a hymn, it's a psalm!"—a simple tribute. A few days before his death he told his son that it was always to come at the end of all editions of his poems. It is a lyric which is on a level with his best work—such lines as

> But such a tide as moving seems asleep,
> Too full for sound and foam—

are of the eternal stamp.

He had felt Robert Browning's death in December, 1889, deeply, but with something of the quiet resignation of age. At this time he amused himself by carving and painting in water-colours. He still went walks and entertained callers, reading many novels, and still working; of *Clarissa Harlowe*, which he read at this time, he said, "I like those great *still* books:" the whole record of his last days is full of quiet interesting talk, not great, but showing a lofty and active mind.

At eighty-two he was still extraordinarily vigorous in body : he would defy his friends to rise twenty times in quick succession from a low chair without touching it with their hands as he could do—he even danced with a child.

Again in 1891 he went a cruise in a yacht and visited Exmouth. He had with him a number of books dealing with the East and Oriental modes of thought which he studied for *Akbar's Dream*.

When he was pressed to write on any particular

subject he used to say, "I cannot: I must write on what I am thinking about, and I have not much time." It is strange how sensitive he still was about little points. He received a complimentary poem from Mr. William Watson, which he acknowledged, adding :—

"If by 'wintry hair' you allude to a tree whose leaves are half gone, you are right, but if you mean white, you are wrong, for I never had a grey hair on my head."

In 1892 he again went for a cruise, and visited Jersey, where his eldest brother was living; the two old poets said their last good-bye.

Good-night, true brother, here, good-morrow there.

On the 29th of June, at Farringford, he received the Communion in his study, from the Rector of Freshwater, and the following day left the Isle of Wight never to return. He went to Aldworth, and on to London, where he visited the Academy and the Natural History Museum. In September he was feeling ill, and when the Master of Balliol came to stay with him he begged that he would not consult him or argue with him on points of philosophy and religion. Jowett answered memorably, "Your poetry has an element of philosophy more to be considered than any regular philosophy in England." Still he was deeply interested in politics and talked with animation and interest.

On the 29th of September he was evidently very ill, and Sir Andrew Clark was telegraphed for; he drove out the same day and said to his son as they passed an accustomed haunt, "I shall never walk there again."

The end drew on with stately tranquillity. On Sunday, 3rd October, he was sinking; but on Monday, very early, he sent for a Shakespeare and some passages were read to him. The same night, with the tender consideration which he always showed, he said to his son, "I make a slave of you."

On Tuesday he wandered a good deal, talked of a journey he was to take, asked if he had not been walking with Gladstone and showing him trees. "Where is my Shakespeare?" he said. "I must have my Shakespeare," and again, "I want to see the sky and the light."

On the Wednesday the fatal tendency to syncope set in, and he lay still, occasionally saying a word or two, and at every sound opening his eyes, looking round the room, and closing them again. Late in the day he gathered himself together, and said one word to the doctor who was attending him: "Death?" The doctor bowed his head—and he said, "That is well." His last words were a blessing to his wife and son. The full moon flooded the room with light, and the watchers waited silently, with awe and love, for the end. He passed away quietly, with one hand clasping his Shakespeare and with the other holding his daughter-in-law's hands—and so he drifted out on the Unknown.

The following day the old clergyman of Lurgashall came to see the peaceful form; the lines of thought were smoothed out of the face by the quiet touch of death The old man raised his hands and said, " Lord Tennyson, God has taken you who made you a prince of men—farewell."

He was buried in Westminster Abbey on the 12th of October, the pall being borne by twelve of the most eminent men in England, many of them his own intimate friends. He lies next to Robert Browning, and in front of the Father of English song.

Lady Tennyson survived him until 1896, having entered her 84th year.

CHAPTER VI

THERE is no need of complex analysis in attempting to draw the character of the great Poet. One of his friends said of him that he was the most transparent human being it is possible to conceive. In ordinary cases it may be roughly said that the child is father of the man, but of Tennyson it may be truly affirmed that the child *was* the man; he was, in fact, the *"imperishable child;"* his simplicity, his modesty, were childish virtues, matured but always childlike; his very faults, his self-absorption, his sensitiveness, his shyness were the faults of childhood. A lady has told me how she once went to call on the Tennysons, whom she hardly knew, and sate for a quarter of an hour with Mrs. Tennyson, during which time Tennyson came three times into the room, as though oblivious of her presence, to grumble over a can of water which he had put out for himself having been poured away by one of the servants. As a rule, advancing years, if they teach a man nothing else, teach him to dissemble; but Tennyson was always himself. He was, said a friend, the only man he knew who habitually thought aloud; he never appears to have suffered from the temptation, the force of which is indefinitely increased by the conditions of modern society, by the rapid circulation of fashion, by the searching glare of public opinion—the temptation to conform oneself, superficially at all events, to the ordinary type. The circumstances of Tennyson's life made it easy for him to follow the bent of his own individuality, and it may be doubted whether his aloofness from ordinary aims and his freedom from the sordid cares which beset humanity were altogether wholesome influences: it must be remembered, however, that though unworldly he was not unpractical. He was a remarkably good man of business, and exacted his due with stern common-sense; so that it may be said that the practical faculties were more in abeyance than absent.

Coventry Patmore gives an interesting description of him :—

"Tennyson is like a great child, very simple and very much self-absorbed. I never heard him make a remark of his own which was worth repeating, yet I always left him with a mind and heart enlarged. In any other man his incessant dwelling upon trifles concerning himself, generally small injuries—real or imaginary—would be very tiresome. He had a singular incapacity for receiving at first hand, and upon its own merits, any new idea. He pooh-poohed my views on architecture when I first put them before him; but some time afterwards Emerson praised them to him very strongly, and the next time I saw Tennyson he praised them strongly too, but without any allusion to his former speech of them."

Two characteristics which appear at first sight inconsistent certainly existed side by side in Tennyson; the first a superficial vanity and self-absorption combined with a true and deep modesty of nature.

He combined, I believe, the modesty of a child with the vanity of a child. He was proud of his accomplishments, never of himself. He had no objection to praising his own poetry. "Not bad that, Fitz?" he used to say to FitzGerald after reading or quoting some favourite line of his own. The truth was that this vanity was more superficial than real. He was so simple-minded that it did not occur to him not to praise his own work if he approved of it, where a more calculating man would have hesitated to say what he was feeling. And he undoubtedly took a modest view of his own powers. "I am a modest man," he said to Thackeray, "and always more or less doubtful of my efforts in any line;"—and his deference to criticism proves this.

On the other hand, he resented deeply and bitterly any depreciation of his work. Even his most intimate friends did not dare to hint disapproval of his works; the deepest affection would not have stood the strain of such a demand.

But he was truly and innately modest about his own character; deeply conscious of imperfection and weakness and sin, for all his honours, he might have said sincerely, to the end of his life, "I am small and of no reputation," for this was what he felt in the sight of God.

As he wrote once to a friend who asked him to be godfather to a child, "I only hope that he will take a better model than his namesake to shape his life by."

I do not imagine that Tennyson's intellectual force was pre-eminently great or that his knowledge was very profound; of technical philosophy, for instance, he said, "I have but a gleam of Kant, and have hardly turned a page of Hegel." The high results that he achieved were largely due to the fact that his interests were limited, and that he was able to devote himself, without any sense of monotony or tedium, entirely to his creative work. Most capable natures require a certain change of intellectual work; the impulse for such natures to labour in new fields is strong, and is increased by the difficulty that men of active intellectual power often feel in keeping closely to one particular species of composition. But this seems not to have been the case with Tennyson. From first to last he

never faltered; he realised early in life that his
work was to be poetry, and though he passed
through moods of dark discouragement, almost
eclipse, yet he never suspended his ideal, and,
moreover, he subordinated all his other work to his
poetical work.

He possessed the poetical temperament almost
to perfection. He had, first, the wholesome in-
sight of genius. Carlyle said of him that "Alfred
had always a grip at the right side of any question."
He had no strong metaphysical grasp, and the subtleties that are so apt to trip the feet of the eager
minute intellect on the threshold were practically
non-existent for him. He saw right to the heart of
a matter, and with a common-sense that was in itself
of the nature of genius, he was able to detect the
typical human view of greater problems, to anticipate the precise angle at which the ray of a great
thought strikes the average human mind. The result was that he had a unique power of saying
things that seemed to sum up and consecrate the
deeper experiences of man. An attempt will be
made later to estimate his religious position; but
it will be enough here to say that it was from the
first a simple one and grew simpler every year. He
had a supreme power of seeing the point, and of dis-
entangling what is accidental and superficial from
what is permanent and essential. In his treatment
of nature this is particularly observable.

Professor Sidgwick pointed out that Wordsworth's view of nature is in one respect a
superficial one ; that he interpreted the external
aspects of nature, the way in which tree, flower,
river and plain strike on the eye, the way in which
the bird's song, the ripple of the stream, or the
querulous wind, appeal to the ear, and through the
avenue of sense touch the heart; but, though
acutely alive to sensorial impressions, Tennyson
went deeper, and approached Nature through her
scientific aspects as well. He discerned, beneath
the smiling surface of plain and hill, the unplumbed
depths of the molten tides. Where Wordsworth
saw the bountiful lavishness of Nature in the leafy
forest gemmed with life, the meadow starred with
daffodils, Tennyson found material for dark and
troubled thought in the desperate waste of Nature,
her heedless profusion, the capacity of humanity to
multiply itself,—"the torrent of babies," as he said
with grim humour. Where Wordsworth saw the
stars as parts of the human environment, the lamps
of night, the sentinels of dewy peace, Tennyson's
thought climbed dizzily into the vast tracts of space,
among the "brushes of fire, beelike swarms" of
worlds. Science and especially astronomy were subjects of perennial attraction to Tennyson ; to Wordsworth they were a profanation, a materialising of
ethereal thoughts. The latter drew strong fortifica-
tions round the province of poetry and feared the

invasion of science as he might have feared the attack of a ruthless foe. Tennyson boldly crossed the frontier and annexed for ever the province of science to the domains of poetry.

Hence came the extraordinary influence of Tennyson over the more active intellects of his era. New thoughts of bewildering intensity, new prospects of intense significance were opening on every side. The danger to be feared was the seclusion of poetry in a world of unreal emotion and elementary sensation. But Tennyson by his courageous attitude proved that there is no danger to poetry in the awakening of wider vision, in the more accurate definition of the scientific law. Science, he showed, could touch the chords of deeper mysteries, and, far from defining the mind of God and confining it within narrower limits, it brought the reverent spirit no nearer to the solution of the eternal riddle, but only made the data richer and more complex.

The Greeks represented Iris, the rainbow messenger of the gods, as the daughter of wonder; and to Tennyson the patient investigation of the principles and conditions of life, instead of diminishing the divine wonder, deepened and intensified it.

It was the same with his treatment of humanity. Tennyson, unlike most poets, felt a deep and absorbing interest in the details of practical politics. The defence of his country, the extension of the franchise, were not to him mere hard distasteful

facts, things likely to disturb the balance of the
poetical faculty, but problems on which he thought
deeply and spoke eagerly. For instance, he said
once fiercely that he could almost wish England to
be invaded by France that he might have the pleasure
of tearing an invader limb from limb.

It seems clear that his acceptance of his peerage
was in part at all events dictated by a deep-seated
desire to have a hand in practical politics ; and thus
though in the poems in which he touched directly
on politics—a fault into which in later life he sometimes fell—he mistakes the quality of poetical
substance, yet in the earlier utterances on freedom,
and in those poems where he indicates political
principles, there is nothing fantastic or unpractical
in his grip ; he does not vaguely flounder in a region
where he felt bound to have views, but speaks out
of the fulness of the heart on matters which were
not to him questions of academical opinion but of
deep and vital enthusiasm.

But all this might have been ineffective if it had
not been for his magical power of language. His
technical mastery of his art will be discussed elsewhere, but from the point of view of a conversational-
ist Tennyson had an extraordinary faculty of finding
the *mot propre*, of summing up a situation in the
tersest and most expressive fashion. His friends
thought him one of the most impressive of talkers,
and there is hardly a story about him, where the

ipsissima verba are given, whether it is a humorous comment, or a dignified reflection, or a picturesque statement, which does not possess a peculiar and weighty quality, a homely appropriateness, an unexpected juxtaposition which could only be attained by one who had a forcible vocabulary at his command, and, and, what is more, within his reach.

For instance, he said to his friend Locker-Lampson, as they sate together, miserably cramped in the top gallery of a small blazing and glaring Parisian theatre: "Locker, this is like being stuck on a spike over hell." Another story may be given in the words of his old friend FitzGerald: "We were stopping before a shop in Regent Street where were two figures of Dante and Goethe. I (I suppose) said, 'What is there in old Dante's Face that is missing in Goethe's?' And Tennyson (whose profile then had certainly a remarkable likeness to Dante's) said, 'The Divine.'"

Again, when in *The Lotos-Eaters* he wrote, describing the infinite variety of streams in the island, of the stream that leaps from a precipice so high that it is entirely disintegrated in its fall and reaches the ground like fine rain,—

> A land of streams! some, like a downward smoke,
> Slow-dropping veils of *thinnest lawn*. . . .

some critic found fault with him for going to the stage for his descriptions, saying that a revolving wreath of loose lawn was the device used in theatres

to produce the illusion of a waterfall. Tennyson
of course had not the least idea that this was so.
But the anecdote shows that he had an extraordinary
power of catching a resemblance and fixing an
impression by the one appropriate word.

There is an amusing story, related by the
Rev. H. Fletcher of Grasmere, who accompanied
Matthew Arnold and Tennyson on a walk in the
Lake country. They came out on a high brow; at
their feet far below lay a great expanse of yellow
mountain pasture, in which a flock of brown-
fleeced sheep were feeding. Matthew Arnold
made several interesting but far-fetched comparisons
of an elaborate kind. "No," said Tennyson, "it
looks like nothing but a great blanket, full of fleas."

To illustrate his forcible directness of speech we
may quote an incident recorded in the *Life*.
Some girl in his presence spoke of a marriage, lately
arranged between two acquaintances of her own, as
a "penniless" marriage. Tennyson glared, rum-
maged in his pocket, produced a penny and slapped
it down before her saying, "There, I give you that!
for that is the god you worship."

Again, to J. R. Green, after a stimulating conversation, the Poet said solemnly, "You're a jolly,
vivid man—and I'm glad to have known you;
you're as vivid as lightning."

Again he was reading *Lycidas* aloud to some
friends in 1870. When he had done, a girl present said

that she had never read *Paradise Lost.* "Shameless daughter of your age," said the Bard.

The above stories, though the thoughts are not exactly conspicuous for brilliance, show a marked power of expressing vivid thought in a salient image.

His impressiveness of speech was no doubt assisted by the undoubted majesty and stateliness of the Poet's personal appearance. It was not only the lofty stature, the domed head, in which he resembled Pericles and Walter Scott, the dark complexion, the eloquent eye, the noble lines drawn by age and experience in the face, but there was a certain pontifical solemnity, a regal deliberation, a rough-hewn dignity, in no sense assumed, which lent weight and majesty to all he said and did. He possessed the natural kingliness that Aristotle attributed to the magnanimous man. In whatever rank of life Tennyson had been born, however grotesque a calling he had pursued, he would have had this unconscious weight in all that he did or said. It is hard to give instances of this particular quality, because by overawing those who passed under its influence it is apt to be subtly felt, and to compel a deference willingly given, rather than to create situations where it is specially evoked. The dignified man has seldom need to defend himself against indignity.

One who knew him well tells me that in later

years it was impossible to deny that, in spite of his obvious desire to be courteous to strangers, he was yet undeniably formidable to a preternatural degree. It was not only the prestige of his fame, because there have been abundance of great men whom in private life it has been impossible to fear. But a sort of awful majesty enveloped Tennyson. His enormous size, the stateliness of his walk, his slow sonorous voice, his noble head with its mass of hair, and the strange peering look, slowly brought to bear upon his interlocutor, all heightened the feeling of personal awe. He was in manner simplicity itself; but in his case this simplicity did not make him more accessible; it only gave the feeling that he would express exactly what he felt whether it was approval or disapproval, encouragement or censure [1]; his greatness made it impossible to meet him on the equal terms which he no doubt expected and assumed to exist; and he was consequently extremely disconcerting to people of shy or highly strung temperament.

Even Jowett, the subtle fencer with words, the refrigerator of timid conversationalists, was by no means at his ease with Tennyson; or rather he was very much on his good behaviour, like a schoolboy with a master who is mainly good-tempered

[1] Mrs. Oliphant relates that Tennyson, in his own house, after listening in silence to an interchange of amiable compliments between herself and Mrs. Tennyson, said abruptly, " *What liars you women are!* "

G

but of uncertain mood; he was tentative, amiable, nervous under the genial but highly flavoured banter with which the Bard plied him; he was complimentary, anxious to avert a social crisis—and if this was the case with an old and valued friend, what must it have been with younger and more sensitive admirers.

The Poet possessed in a remarkable degree the power of attachment in friendship not less than in love. But he rather demanded affection than gave it; and it is plain that his absorption in his work and his active interest in the details of life saved him from much suffering. It is strange that the writer of one of the greatest and completest of elegies should not, in respect to his relations with human beings, give the impression of being a "man of sorrows and acquainted with grief." His affections were essentially of a tranquil kind. His friends found him invariably the same, but it may be doubted whether in their absence he thought very much about them. The story of his rupture with Coventry Patmore will illustrate this. When Coventry Patmore's first wife died, the two poets being close friends—indeed Coventry Patmore divided his friends into two classes, of which one was "Tennyson" and the other was "the rest"—Tennyson neither went to see him, nor wrote him a single line of sympathy on the sad event. Mrs. Tennyson, indeed, thinking that Mrs. Patmore's illness must have entailed heavy expense on Patmore, and that he was a poor man, arranged an application to the Premier for some bounty or pension to assist him at a crisis so sad. This Tennyson signed, and it is the only indication of interest that he manifested. Coventry Patmore wrote and asked him to come and see him ; of which letter Tennyson took no notice, saying many years after that it had never reached him.

For nearly twenty years there was a complete rupture of relations which had been extraordinarily intimate. Tennyson seems occasionally to have expressed a mild wonder that Patmore had given him up, but it did not extend so far as to induce him to write a letter asking if anything was amiss. Patmore is perhaps to blame for not having unravelled the matter further, but he certainly had reason for thinking that Tennyson's conduct was unfeeling.

In any case the two attached friends, the poet of Friendship and the poet of Domestic Love, fell into an entire silence which lasted for twenty years, for a misunderstanding which a letter from either might have dispelled.

Such a story, though it is not inconsistent with an affectionate temperament, gives no hint of the intense personal devotion, the hungering eagerness for sight and speech which are generally characteristic of affectionate natures. One sees the child here as all through. A child can be truly loving, irresistibly impelled to create and enjoy an atmosphere of affection about itself—but without

very deep attachment, and needing to live surrounded by looks and words of love rather than to
be slow in maturing love and affection, and inconsol-
able without the presence of particular objects of
the desire of the heart.

The natural melancholy of Tennyson's temperament must here be noted. He was probably, like
most melancholy men, happier more often than he
knew; he thawed, mostly in the evening, under the
influences of conversation, wine and tobacco, into an
irresistibly genial and sociable mood; but it was of
the nature of distraction; and left to himself the
spirit fell back with singular helplessness down the
rugged ascent into the dark pool. There hung a
cloud over him from day to day, say those who knew
him best. He often sighed, he often complained of
his own unhappiness. But it must often have been,
as Gray said, of his own depression, a good easy sort
of a state, and well suited for the exercise of poetical
meditation: a conscious burden, no doubt, but not
necessarily an uncongenial atmosphere for poetry
to rise and flower in.

Another characteristic trait of Tennyson was his
extraordinary sensitiveness. He used to say that
his skin was typical of his mental temperament,
that a fleabite would spread an inch over the surface. His sensitiveness to criticism was abnormal.
He used to admit that he was indifferent to praise
and that he could not bear blame. An adverse

criticism was to him a personal matter. He was
apt to attribute it to definite malignity, or to in-
tolerable ignorance.   A friend tells me that he
went from the house of a dignitary of the Church
to stay with Tennyson; and he repeated some criticism that had been made by his host on *Queen
Mary*, which he had pronounced to be a stately
poem but unsuitable to the stage.   Tennyson swept
aside the praise and settled upon the criticism with
extraordinary persistence.   Again and again he re-
verted to it with a somewhat painful iteration.
The following day when the guest departed Tennyson came to say good-bye, and with great solemnity
said, "Tell your friend—the *Canon*" (with ironical
emphasis) "that he doesn't know what the drama
is!"   Again a friend of his tells me that when she
was staying at Farringford, some one brought there
a school magazine in which there was a disparaging
allusion to the Poet.   She says that it was most
painful to see how for days the words burned in his
mind like a poisoned wound; no matter what subject
was started, no matter how much interested he
himself became in pursuing a train of thought, he
always came back to the same grievance.   No
amount of influence with other minds it seemed
could atone for what " these young gentlemen"
had said.   Such stories could be multiplied indefinitely.   But he was true to his principles in
the matter, treating others as he desired to be

treated, and though a master of personal invective, as is shown by the lines on Bulwer Lytton, he resolutely suppressed it in his writings, except in an impersonal way. The picture of the pious company promoter in *Sea Dreams* is sketched by the hand of a powerful satirist. He hated spitefulness above all things. He was told that the celebrated lines in *Maud*, about the coal mine, had given offence to worthy owners ; he replied with the utmost indignation, "Sooner than wound any one in such a spiteful fashion, I would consent never to write again ; yea, to have my hand cut off at the wrist."

Undoubtedly the sheltered atmosphere in which he lived tended to increase these characteristics. Guarded from the world by an intensely loyal and loving wife, and by a son whose filial devotion was more of a passion than a sentiment, he missed the equality of criticism which might, as with a subtle file, have worn down the angles of personality. There was something, too, as I have said, majestic and unapproachable about his personal dignity which was apt to compel admiring deference. Thus, like royal personages, he passed the later years of his life in a somewhat unreal atmosphere of subtle subservience. But it must be added that there were few people who could have borne the adulation which was so freely lavished on him without far greater enervation of character. His

house became a place of pilgrimage, and his natural
simplicity led him to talk easily of himself, his
tastes and prejudices.   No doubt the one thing
desired by all pilgrims is that the object of their
devotion should tell them something about himself;
and one of the reasons which makes pilgrimages to
see a great man so disappointing is that the hero
so rarely talks on the one subject that brings his
visitors to the place.   But this was not Tennyson's
way.   He was generally ready to read his poems
and to talk about them.   Probably there is no poet
about whom so many authentic traditions exist as
to lines which he praised as "the best he ever
wrote."   Carried away by the impulse of the
moment, and sincerely approving of some line which
was under discussion, the Bard, with an almost
Oriental instinct of hospitality, fell easily into a vein
which he knew would delight his hearers.

Tennyson was, in a way, extraordinarily shy;
an eager questioner, a timorous child, a nervous
visitor would freeze him into gloomy silence;
on the other hand with people of tranquil
and self-possessed manner, who talked easily and
naturally, and who showed decorous deference
without inconvenient curiosity, he was expansive,
humorous and natural.   He alternated between
what appeared to be excessive rudeness, when he
was in fact only thinking aloud—as when he asked
a child who was introduced to him why his hand

felt like a toad [1]—and the most tender and considerate courtesy; it all depended upon his mood; sometimes he was a model of noble deference to old people, whether venerable or not. Yet O. W. Holmes, then aged nearly eighty, after a visit to Tennyson, gently complained to a friend, "He did not realise, I think, that I am an old man, and accustomed to being treated kindly."

Speaking once of the secret of oratory he said, "I am never the least shy before great men. Each of them has a personality for which he or she is responsible; but before a crowd which consists of many personalities, of which I know nothing, I am infinitely shy. The great orator cares nothing about all this. I think of the good man, and the bad man, and the mad man, that may be among them, and can say nothing. *He* takes them all as one man. *He* sways them as one man."

Another characteristic demands a word. Tennyson had in conversation a virile freshness which led him to speak in the plainest terms on subjects which are seldom discussed in detail in ordinary society. The same vigorous humanity which made him say that any port which was

---

[1] No doubt he had a line of Herrick's in his mind from *Another Grace for a Child:*—

> Here a little child I stand
> Heaving up my either hand
> *Cold as paddocks though they be*, etc.

"sweet and black and strong enough" was good enough for him, made his talk on occasions Rabelaisian from its plainness. This fact is worth mentioning because in his poems he is like Virgil, delicate almost to the verge of prudery; though such a poem as *Lucretius* showed plainly enough that this delicacy was the result of deliberate theory and not of natural temperament. There can be no better proof that this outspoken tendency was real frankness, and untainted by the least shadow of prurience, than the fact that there is no poet ancient or modern who could be put with such supreme and entire confidence in the hands of the most maidenly of readers; and that the instinct for purity was so strong as to be held almost to emasculate his work. When Tennyson wrote of "the poisonous honey brought from France" a well-known writer whose moral outlook is less austere retorted by speaking of the "Laureate's domestic treacle."

Tennyson rated humour very high; in a letter to his future wife he said solemnly that she would find it in most great writers—even in the Gospel of Christ. Among his own writings the dialect poems show how strong and genuine a vein of humour he himself possessed. He was fond of amusing anecdotes and told them well; but he had as well a strong vein of original and native picturesqueness of a humorous kind in conversation. What could be more delightful than his comment on a novel

of Miss Yonge's, which he read with profound
absorption, suffering nothing to distract him? At
last he closed the book and laid it down, saying
with an air of inexpressible relief, "I see land!
Harry *is* going to be confirmed."

He had an immense admiration for Miss Austen
as a writer. He once made a pilgrimage to Lyme
Regis, to study the scene of *Persuasion;* one
of the company, a person of well-regulated mind,
made some allusion to the Duke of Monmouth.
"Don't talk to me of Monmouth," said Tennyson
sternly, "but show me the *exact spot* where Louisa
Musgrove fell!"

But the most humorous effects of his conversation
were produced by a certain mystic solemnity of
phrase or grim exaggeration, greatly enhanced by
his stateliness of enunciation.

Travelling in Switzerland he was much annoyed
by a terrible smell which prevailed at a spot from
which there was a view of a famous waterfall. He
said pathetically that he was painfully sensitive to
such impressions, and that the atrocious smell and
the magnificent prospect would be for ever insepar-
ably connected in his mind—adding sententiously,
"This is an age of lies, and it is also an age of stinks."

At the sight of the tail of a great glacier loaded
with dirty débris, he said, "That glacier is a filthy
thing; it looks as if a thousand London seasons
had passed over it."

When the Metaphysical Society was founded in 1869, the Poet said, *à propos* of a somewhat acrid discussion which had taken place, " Modern Society ought at all events to have taught men to separate light from heat," words which were adopted as the motto of the society.

On one occasion, says the legend, Tennyson was walking with a friend, and, stumbling in getting over a stile, fell to the ground ;—it seems that though muscularly strong he was always clumsy —his friend, knowing his dislike both of being helped and also of having such incidents witnessed, walked on a few paces, and turning round saw that Tennyson had made no effort to rise, but was lying with his face extended over a little muddy pool by the hedgerow, overgrown with duck-weed.   Thinking that the Poet had dropped something in his fall, and was looking for it, he returned.   Tennyson raised himself slowly on his hands and knees, and turned a face, dim with rapt and serious contemplation, upon him, saying in a deep tone, "T——, what an imagination God Almighty has ! "   This exclamation was drawn from him by the sight of the little pool, with its myriad and dainty forms of infusorial life and beauty, all fresh from the mind of God.

In 1887 he went to see his eldest brother Frederick, who was greatly occupied with the phenomena of Spiritualism, and who tried to persuade the Laureate to go seriously into the question. The Poet heard him patiently, and then said with great emphasis, "I am convinced that God and the ghosts of men would choose something other than mere table-legs through which to speak to the heart of man."

On another occasion he said with humorous sadness that the sense of religior in England was of a very precarious order. "The general English view of God is as of an immeasurable clergyman."

He was very fond of the story of the Duke of Wellington, who was piloted over a crowded crossing by an enthusiastic stranger. The Duke put his hand into his pocket as if about to reward his benefactor, when the stranger said hysterically that the only reward he desired was to be allowed to shake the hand of the great conqueror. To which the Duke replied, "Don't be a d——d fool!" Commenting on this Tennyson said that the answer was almost as great in its way as the battle of Waterloo—adding, "A Frenchman would have answered, 'Mais, oui! on m'appelle le grand!'"

He was always very indignant over the desire to invade the privacy of great men. He said once to Mr. Palgrave that if he had in his hands an autobiography of Horace, the only copy in existence, he would burn it; Sir Henry Taylor, in his *Autobio-*

graphy, quotes a delightful undated letter, written by Mrs. Cameron about the year 1860, which contains a forcible diatribe of Tennyson's on the subject :—

"He was very violent with the girls on the subject of the rage for autographs. He said he believed every crime and every vice in the world were connected with the passion for autographs and anecdotes and records ; that the desiring anecdotes and acquaintance with the lives of great men was treating them like pigs, to be ripped open for the public ; that he knew he himself should be ripped open like a pig ; that he thanked God Almighty with his whole heart and soul that he knew nothing, and that the world knew nothing of Shakespeare but his writings ; and that he thanked God Almighty that he knew nothing of Jane Austen, and that there were no letters preserved either of Shakespeare's or Jane Austen's, that they had not been ripped open like pigs. Then he said that the post for two days had brought *him* no letters, and that he thought there was a sort of syncope in the world as to him and his fame."

The unconscious transition in the last remark to the egotistic vein is as characteristic as the violence of the earlier words.

I have sometimes wondered whether the simile at the beginning of *Sea Dreams* was dictated by a subtle sense of humour or no. After describing the slender savings of the city clerk, so precariously invested, he adds :—

As the *little thrift*
Trembles in perilous places o'er the deep.

Neither was he averse to practical humour. An American visitor describes how he first saw Tennyson driving in a small pony-carriage with one of his grandchildren; they had exchanged hats; and the child sate with his head enveloped in the huge black wide-awake that was so characteristic of the Poet, while Tennyson wore perched at the top of his great head with its flowing curls a small straw sailor's hat. He made no attempt to change or lay aside this head-dress, and conducted the interview without embarrassment or loss of gravity.

Again, in 1879, the Laureate met the present Queen at Mrs. Greville's in Chester Square. The Princess asked Tennyson to read her the *Welcome to Alexandra.* Tennyson did so, and when he had finished, the fact of the reading his own complimentary poem aloud to the Princess struck him as so ludicrous, that he dropped the book and fell into uncontrollable laughter, which was cordially re-echoed by the Princess herself.

Such, then, was the man—simple, wise, laborious, impressive, trenchant, outspoken, yet sensitive withal, self-absorbed and moody; with the heart of a child, the vision of a poet, and the faith of a mystic, in a mighty, rugged, vigorous frame, full of strong animal and human impulse; living a life that tended to develop both the good and the evil of his temperament; for the seclusion and ease that makes divine dreams possible is also a soil in which the frailties, passions and vanities of human nature burgeon and flower. "Prophecy," said George Eliot, "is of all the mistakes we commit the most gratuitous;" prophecy in the pluperfect subjunctive—what might have been—is more gratuitous still. But FitzGerald, who knew and grasped the strength and weakness of Tennyson's character, was strongly of opinion that Tennyson's life had not had an entirely wholesome effect upon him— and no one had better opportunities of realising the dangers of the sheltered life than FitzGerald.

The latter, writing in 1876 (24th October) to Mrs. Kemble, and speaking of the captain of his sailing-boat, a majestic and tranquil personage, whom he much admired and respected, he said, " I thought that both Tennyson and Thackeray were inferior to him in respect of Thinking of Themselves. When Tennyson was telling me of how the *Quarterly* abused him (humorously too), and desirous of knowing why one did not care for his later works, etc., I thought that if he had lived an active Life, as Scott and Shakespeare; or even ridden, shot, drunk, and played the Devil, as Byron, he would have done much more, and talked about it much less. 'You know,' said Scott to Lockhart, 'that I don't care a curse about what I write,' and one sees he did not. I don't believe it was far otherwise with Shakespeare. Even old Wordsworth, wrapped up in his Mountain mists, and proud as he was, was above all this vain Disquietude: proud, not vain, was he: and that a Great Man (as Dante) has some right to be—but not to care what the Coteries say."

This is a charming and subtle piece of criticism —but probably only contains a half-truth. It is too much in the line of Carlyle's dictum that Tennyson was a life-guardsman spoiled by writing poetry. But there are plenty of life-guardsmen, and we cannot sacrifice a poet. A price must be paid for everything; and though we may not think Tennyson's attitude entirely manly or philosophical, we may be thankful for the life, which at the cost of some superficial pettiness, was at all events deliberately pursued, with a high sense of vocation, and the fruit of which was so abundant and so gracious.

CHAPTER VII

TENNYSON'S creed was a simple one, and grew simpler as he grew older. The two cardinal points of his faith were his belief in God, and his belief in the immortality of man. On these great thoughts the life of his soul was nourished,—the Fatherhood of God, and the Life of the World to come.

He said once, in memorable words, to Mr. Knowles, "There's a something that watches over us; and our individuality endures: that's my faith, and that's all my faith."

He seems to have been brought up in a simple, Christian, almost Calvinistic creed, and there is little evidence at any period of agonising doubt, any uprooting of the vital principles of religion. If there was any such fuller testimony it is buried in sacred silence; perhaps the conflict was fought out in his own heart. Possibly the letters to Arthur Hallam, which were destroyed after the death of the latter, would have contained some details of the inner struggle, if such struggle there were; but

H   (105)

more probably there was only a gradual transition of thought. His own feeling about the preservation and making public of such records was so strong that we must acquiesce in the destruction of these valuable letters; though we may be allowed to regret it in no inquisitive spirit, but because it might have helped those whose belief was less firmly based to study reverently the processes by which so strong and vital a faith was arrived at.

There is extant an unfinished prayer, which he composed as a boy, which leaves no doubt that he accepted Christian dogmas in the most mechanical and literal way; but when he went to Cambridge the question was brought before him in a more personal manner.

The most interesting autobiographical document among the earlier poems is the *Supposed Confessions,* so the somewhat cumbrous title runs, *of a Second-rate Sensitive Mind not in Unity with Itself.* This poem, which belongs to the 1830 volume, was not reprinted till 1872, when it appeared in the *Juvenilia* with seventeen lines omitted.

We note, in the first place, that this is the most definitely Christian poem which Tennyson ever wrote; it speaks of the Birth and Passion of Christ in terms which imply if not a belief, at least a desirous hope in the doctrines of the Incarnation and the Atonement. Probably Tennyson would have resented the too close application of the poem to his own case; indeed there is a passage in the poem in which the soliloquist speaks of his dead mother which looks like a deliberate attempt to give an environment not his own to the poem. But on the other hand it has an *intimité* which makes it impossible to regard it in any light but the autobiographical; such a poem cannot be simply dramatic, and indeed in Tennyson's case the dramatic impulse had hardly even begun to flower at the time when it was written. His suppression of the poem, too, appears to indicate that he felt it, with his extreme love of privacy, to be too urgent a self-revelation, that he had allowed himself "to tear his heart before the crowd."

The difficulty which meets the reader of the poem at the outset is this: what is the precise catastrophe that is indicated? In words which seem to deplore a loss of faith the speaker appears to reiterate and affirm the conviction that faith is the one thing left him in a hopeless world. Perhaps it may be held to be a revelation of the process by which a mechanical faith becomes vital; the supposed speaker seems to say that his faith is deserting him, and that he cannot revivify it; he appears to be in the condition of one who has held an unquestioning creed, which has never been put to the supreme test, has never encountered a crisis such as might lead the believer to find that such a faith was not enough to meet, with ample reserves, the darkest experience of life. Then there falls one of the "moods of misery unutterable," which sometimes beset an imaginative nature of hitherto tranquil experiences on the threshold of real life; such a nature, living vividly, if not happily, in the present, and still more in the future, realises how rapidly both present and future become merged in the past, how incredibly short life is when compared with the infinite dreams in which the hopeful mind has indulged; the thought of death and the dark after-world rises in unimagined horror; the world seems one gloomy necropolis—" Mixta senum et juvenum densentur funera; *nullum Saeva caput Proserpina fugit,*" as the old poet said.

Then the faith which has been tranquil, mechanical, customary, rings hollow; it cannot bear the strain; and the poem is a cry for a faith which may gleam and sparkle like a sunlit sea beyond the dark tracts of death.

> Oh, teach me yet
> Somewhat before the heavy clod
> Weighs on me, and the busy fret
> Of that sharp-headed worm begins
> In the gross blackness underneath.

The mood struggles, as it were, to the very threshold of faith and finds the door shut; then the impulse suddenly flags, the dreary cloud descends again upon the soul.

Not only is the motive of the poem not charac·

teristic of the writer, but the very scheme of rhyme
and tone of language are un-Tennysonian; long
sentences of dubious structure shape themselves
independent of the crisp form of the metre. The
images, the expressions are sometimes characteristic,
but one cannot help wondering whether, if the
poem had been sedulously withheld from publication, and had long after appeared anonymously, the
most perspicuous critic would have traced the
authorship unhesitatingly. One can imagine indeed
a critic of the advanced theological German school
declaring emphatically against the genuineness of
the poem on both internal and external grounds.

Still it contains passages or rather expressions of
rare and singular beauty; and as a window into the
writer's soul it is of inexpressible interest.

I think it is clear that after this date his mind
broke gradually away to a certain extent from
precise dogmatic Christian doctrine; or rather that,
as his faith in essentials grew more vital, he rested
less in dogmatic religion than in the deepest and
simplest truths. I imagine that he looked upon a
dogmatic symbol as he might have looked upon a
piece of parliamentary drafting, as containing a
truth or a principle but involved in subtle legal
definition, and not in itself inspiring or fruitful for
the ordinary mind.

That he regarded the Person and teaching of
Christ with the deepest reverence is clear enough.

He wrote in 1839 to his future wife, that he was staying with "an old friend" at Mablethorpe. "He and his wife," he writes, "are two perfectly honest Methodists. When I came, I asked her after news, and she replied, 'Why, Mr. Tennyson, there is only one piece of news that I know, that Christ died for *all* men.' And I said to her: 'That is old news and good news and new news;' wherewith the good woman seemed satisfied. I was half yesterday reading anecdotes of Methodist ministers, and liking to read them too . . . and of the teaching of Christ, that purest light of God."

Long after he spoke of Christ as "that union of man and woman, sweetness and strength." But he was not a habitual attendant upon the worship of the Church, and it is significant to note that in his closing years (1892), when he received the Communion in his study at Freshwater, he solemnly quoted his own words, put into Cranmer's mouth, before he partook :—

> It is but a communion, not a mass :
> No sacrifice, but a life-giving feast ;

impressing upon the clergyman that he could not partake of it at all, unless it were administered in that sense.

Once indeed a visitor ventured to ask him, as they were walking in the garden, what he thought of our Saviour   He said nothing at first, then he

stopped by a beautiful flower, and said, "What the
sun is to that flower, Jesus Christ is to my soul. He
is the Sun of my soul."

Tennyson said that Christianity, with its Divine
morality, but without the central figure of Christ,
the Son of Man, would become cold; and that it
is fatal for religion to lose its warmth; that *The
Son of Man* was the most tremendous title possible;
that the forms of Christian religion would alter, but
that the Spirit of Christ would grow from more to
more "in the roll of the ages;" that his line,

Ring in the Christ that is to be,

"points to the time when Christianity without
bigotry will triumph, when the controversies of
creeds shall have vanished."

"I am always amazed," he said, "when I read
the New Testament at the splendour of Christ's
purity and holiness, and at His infinite pity."

The above sayings are enough to show the profound reverence with which Tennyson regarded
Christ, as the perfect *exemplar* of humanity. But
the deep mystery of the union of the human and
Divine was evidently a thought which he did not
attempt to fathom, and we may perhaps say that
his mind turned more naturally to the possibility of
the believer's direct union with God than to the
more definite Christian conception of the union
through Christ. It is of course inevitable that

certain aspects of faith should come home with
greater force to some minds than to others, and I
think it is clear that this particular aspect of the
question was not one on which his mind dwelt
serenely and habitually.

We will turn then to the definite side of his faith,
and try to indicate the lines on which it moved.
He seems in those silent years, of which so little
record is left, to have made up his mind that a life
without faith, without religion, was impossible.
As he wrote to his future wife, "What matters it
how much man knows and does if he keep not a
reverential looking upward? He is only the subtlest
beast in the field."

At the same time he seems to have grown to
feel that for him, at all events, the secret did not
lie in the subtleties of religious definition. "The
Almighty will not ask you," he once said, "what
particular form of creed you have held, but 'Have
you been true to yourself, and given in my Name "a
cup of cold water to one of these little ones?"'"

Yet he sometimes seemed to hanker after a more
definite faith; speaking of his friend and neighbour,
W. G. Ward, he said once, "If I had Ward's blind
faith, I should always be happy." He saw, moreover, the necessity of a working system in matters
of religion, and the danger of vagueness. "An
organised religion," he once said, "is the needful
guardian of morality."

Dr. Martineau said that Tennyson's poetry had
"a dissolving influence upon over-definite dogmatic
creeds:" but that he had created, or immeasur-
ably intensified, the susceptibility to religious
reverence.

He studied, particularly after his marriage, the
Bible very closely, and also made himself acquainted
with the chief systems of philosophy. His conclusion was a certain terror of minute scientific
analysis in matters of religion. "Nothing worth
proving can be proven," he said. At the same time
he had the greatest horror of the sacrifice of religion
to reason. "I hate unfaith," he said, "I cannot
endure that men should sacrifice everything at the
cold altar of what with their imperfect knowledge
they choose to call truth and reason." The whole
drift of *In Memoriam* is that humanity will not and

cannot acquiesce in a godless world; and the two
principles by which Tennyson tried to guide his
life were the Fatherhood of God, implying the
possibility of the direct union of the soul with God
—and the hope of immortality.

"My most passionate desire," he said, "is to have
a clearer and fuller vision of God," adding reverently, "I can sympathise with God in my poor
little way." Freewill, he thought, was the intimate
connection between the human and Divine.

"We see," he once said, "the shadow of God in
the world—a distorted shadow. Faith must be our

guide; " again, " The flesh is the vision, the spiritual the only real and true."

Speaking of the character of Arthur in the *Idylls*, he said, " For Arthur and for every one who believes in the Word, however interpreted, the question arises, ' How can I in my little life, in my small measure, and in my limited sphere reflect this highest Ideal?'"

" God reveals himself," he said, " in every individual soul, and my idea of heaven is the perpetual ministry of one soul to another."

It was this intense belief in the Divine principle in the world that made Jowett say of him that " he had a strong desire to vindicate the ways of God to man."

In his belief in the possibility of the union between the human spirit and God, he wrote and thought as a mystic. He believed in prayer, but he recognised that the increasing difficulty in the way of the scientific defining of prayer was the extended knowledge of the laws that prevail in the natural world. In his own life the need of prayer became greater and more urgent, but the forms of prayer became less definite. As Wordsworth wrote :—

> Thought was not, in emotion it expired ;
> No thanks he breathed, he proffered no request.

" Prayer," Tennyson said, " is the opening a sluice between the ocean and the little channel."

No less strong was his perfect faith in personal immortality. Praising Goethe as one of the wisest of men, he quoted with approbation Goethe's words: "I hope I shall never be so weak-minded as to let my belief in a future life be torn from me."

"I can hardly understand," he once said, "how any great, imaginative man, who has deeply lived, suffered, thought and wrought can doubt of the Soul's continuous progress in the after life." "The instinct for another life is a presumption of its truth," he once said.

The letters that he wrote to those suffering under bereavements have the same fervent belief in immortality expressed. To a friend who had lost a son he wrote :—

"My own belief is that the son whom you so loved is not really what we call dead, but more actually living than when alive here."

To Lord Houghton, on the death of his wife, he wrote, "I think I can see, as far as any one can see in this twilight, that the nobler nature does not pass from its individuality when it passes out of this one life."

But this faith was not a vague and dreamlike emotion, but sternly practical. He used to speak of the war of sense and soul, the spreading poison of sin, the transmuting power of repentance, "Motive," he said, "consecrates life."

Speaking of a boy going up to the university he said with great emphasis :—

"A young man ought not to be a bundle of sensations; he ought to have selfless and adventurous heroism, not to shirk responsibilities, to cast aside maudlin and introspective morbidities, to use his powers cheerfully in obedience to the dictates of moral consciousness." "Can he," he added, "battle against bad instincts, can he brave public opinion in the cause of truth?"

Again he said of himself, "I see the nothingness of life, I know its emptiness—but I believe in Love and Virtue and Duty."

He felt, as he grew older, the despondency caused by decreased energy, that despondency which betrayed itself in the pessimism of some of his later poems, but he said, "In my age I have a stronger faith in God and human good even than in youth."

This faith was accompanied by a strong sense of the battle waged within himself with lower instincts. In one of Hallam's early letters to him occurs the passage, "You say pathetically, 'Alas for me, I have more of the beautiful than the good.'" Hallam goes on to say that "the fact that he should recognise this and sorrow over it was in itself an indication of the eventual triumph of the Divine." And this triumph was won. It has been held by those who teach that Art must be followed entirely and solely for its own sake, that Tennyson's art was vitiated by the moral purpose it reveals. The question is not one to be discussed here; but it may be said that Tennyson considered this view to be almost blasphemous, and sacrificing the deeper truth of life to the more superficial.

"Art for art—and *Man's* sake," he said, had always been his principle.

The humility which lay beneath a certain superficial vanity is touchingly illustrated by his pathetic words when his son Hallam, then at school, was seriously ill :—

"God will take him," he said, "pure and good, straight from his mother's lessons. Surely it would be better for him than to grow up such a one as I am."

This, then, was his faith; not the faith that cannot be content without parcelling out its information into scientific sections, but a deep sense of mystery and humility, a firm belief in the great purposes of God for man. "There is no answer," he said, "to these questions except in a quiet *hope* of universal good." He held, too, the conviction that the one thing needful in the world was a deeply rooted vital faith, on which all the aspirations and progress of humanity must be based. "We cannot give up," he said, "the mighty hopes that make us men."

It seems to be claimed, or perhaps hoped, by the

ardent upholders of Tennyson that he is destined
to survive as a religious philosopher and that he
has defined the attitude of Faith to Science, established some invincible position in religion. The
hope is destined to disappointment: Tennyson's
philosophy was probably always considered elementary by the advanced school. Of course, in one
sense, his influence is permanent, as all influence
that is strongly felt at any period of the intellectual
or moral life of a nation is permanent; because it
contained the seed of future development and is
in itself an integral link in the chain; but the
data are different now, and the disposition of the
struggle is changed. Further, Tennyson established
nothing; the most he did was to express with profound emotion, and in language of admirable beauty,
the fact that, as Henry Sidgwick said, there is, or
seems to be, an inalienable modicum of faith which
humanity is bound to retain, and will not be persuaded to reject. But we must face the fact that
even if that faith is universally retained, it may be
that it will embrace a different scheme, and cling
to points which Tennyson considered unessential,
while it abandons what he held to be indubitable.
It may be, we say—for the course of philosophical
discovery is impossible to predict.

But even if Tennyson's axioms should be rejected,
it still may be that his profound sincerity, his
poignant emotion in the presence of the deepest

mysteries, and above all the lucid solemnity, the stately dignity of his language, will continue to make his work a permanent monument of the human spirit; as permanent, that is, as any trophy of the human mind can dare to claim to be.

CHAPTER VIII

I T is interesting to attempt to trace the literary influences and to discuss the writers on which the genius of Tennyson was nurtured. As a child he seems to have read Byron, Thomson, Pope—whom he called " a consummate artist in the lower sense of the term"—and Walter Scott. It is noticeable that many of the early poems are mere Byronic exercises. He improvised hundreds of lines in the style of Pope, and he wrote an early epic in the style of Walter Scott. He was attracted by Thomson's descriptions of nature and wrote with facility in imitation of him. At the age of twelve he wrote a long critical letter to an aunt on the subject of Samson (spelt Sampson) Agonistes, mainly composed of quotations, in which he pronounces Milton a pedant. It is not recorded what his favourite poetical reading was before he went to the university, but he must have read Milton carefully, and the influence of Keats is distinctly traceable in the Cambridge prize poem on Timbuctoo; there are, too, curious traces of the study of Shelley in *The Lover's Tale* of 1833, after which date the direct influence of other poetry on his style seems to have ceased ; he himself stated that in later years nothing that he wrote was consciously imitative.

But from that time to the end of his life a large number of very acute and sympathetic critical dicta on literary matters are recorded.   Mr. Lecky in the interesting reminiscences which he wrote of the poet says that he was an admirable critic, and that he was especially qualified for critical discriminations by his great delicacy of ear and his retentive verbal memory.   Mr. Gladstone called him "a candid, strict and fastidious judge" of literature, and there is little doubt that if he had devoted himself to critical work he would have left eminently sound, sure-footed and discriminating judgments.

The best proof, however, of his knowledge and taste is *The Golden Treasury* of 1861, edited by F. T. Palgrave, who, it is well known, was very largely indebted to the catholic erudition and fine feeling of Tennyson.

It will be interesting to indicate his chief preferences in poetry and to examine his criticisms.   They were mostly delivered in conversation, but it is to be noted that his judgment does not seem to have varied according to his mood, but that he had a constant and formed opinion which was little modified.

He approached literature in the spirit of pure

I

appreciation. He never professed to be a learned student or to have made an exhaustive study of the poetry which he admired. He wrote in 1885 to Dr. Grosart, "I am very unlearned, not only in Spenser but in most of our old poets, and I delight (not being a Bibliophile) rather in the 'consummate flower' of a writer, than in the whole of him, root and all, bad and good together. . . ."

For Shakespeare he had the profoundest admiration, as for a writer almost superhuman, classing him with Æschylus, Dante and Goethe, as "the great Sage poets, great thinkers and great artists." He once quoted as a young man a saying of the historian Hallam that Shakespeare was the "*greatest man.*" FitzGerald demurred to this, and said that he thought such dicta rather peremptory for a philosopher. "Well," said Tennyson, "the man one would wish perhaps to show as a sample of mankind to those in another planet." A little later, "in his weaker moments," he would say that Shakespeare was greater in his sonnets than in his plays—"but he soon returned to the thought which is indeed the thought of all the world." Again he said with solemn deliberateness that "Hamlet was the greatest creation in literature," and that there was one intellectual process in the world of which he could not even entertain an apprehension—the process by which the plays of Shakespeare were produced.

Speaking of individual plays he said that "no one had drawn the true passion of love like Shakespeare;" for inimitably natural talk between husband and wife he would quote the scene between Hotspur and Lady Percy *(King Henry IV.*, Part I.), and would exclaim, "How deliciously playful is that

> 'In faith, I'll break thy little finger, Harry,
> An if thou wilt not tell me all things true.'"

He would say, "There are three repartees in Shakespeare which always bring the tears to my eyes from their simplicity.

"One is in *King Lear*, when Lear says to Cordelia, 'So young and so untender,' and Cordelia lovingly answers, 'So young, my lord, and true.' And in *The Winter's Tale*, when Florizel takes Perdita's hand to lead her to the dance, and says, 'So turtles pair that never mean to part,' and the little Perdita answers, giving her hand to Florizel, 'I'll swear for 'em.' And in *Cymbeline*, when Imogen in tender rebuke says to her husband,

> 'Why did you throw your wedded lady from you?
> Think that you are upon a rock; and now
> Throw me again.'

and Posthumus does not ask forgiveness, but answers, kissing her,

> 'Hang there like fruit, my soul
> Till the tree die.' '

"*King Lear,*" he used to say, "cannot possibly be acted, it is too titanic. . . . This play shows a state of society where men's passions are savage and uncurbed. No play like this anywhere—not even the *Agamemnon*—is so terrifically human."

Again he said, "Actors do not comprehend that Shakespeare's greatest villains, Iago among them, have always a touch of conscience. You see the conscience working—therein lies one of Shakespeare's pre-eminences."

"*Macbeth,*" again he said, with fine perception, "is not as is too often represented, a noisy swash-buckler: he is a full-furnished, ambitious man."

Commenting on Shakespeare's literary style he said that the great Æschylean lines in Shakespeare were often overlooked, instancing

> The burning crest
> Of the old, feeble, and day-wearied sun.

Shakespeare was to him the great interpreter of life in the light of poetry. It is touching to remember that it was the last book he read, on his deathbed. Three days before he died he sent early in the morning for his Shakespeare; his son brought him in Steevens' edition, *Lear, Cymbeline,* and *Troilus and Cressida,* three of his favourite plays; he read a few lines, and asked that more should be read to him. On the next day, when he was wandering a good deal, and talking about a long journey he seemed about to take, he broke off to say, "Where is my Shakespeare? I must have my Shakespeare." On the last day he begged for the book again and lay with his hand resting on it, open, trying to read it ; almost his last recorded words were, "I have opened it." It was thought that this referred to the book, which he had opened at the lines, already quoted,

> "Hang there like fruit, my soul
> Till the tree die."

The book was buried with him, and lies next his heart.

Milton he called "Supreme in the material sublime," and said that he was greater than Virgil. *Lycidas,* he said, was a test of poetic instinct. He used to praise Milton's similes, especially

> As when far off at sea a fleet descried
> Hangs in the clouds, by equinoctial winds
> Close sailing from Bengala— (Bk. ii. 634)

saying, "What simile was ever so *vast* as this ?"

As an instance of a liquid line he would quote

> And in the ascending scale
> Of Heaven, the stars that usher evening rose,

adding, "This last line is lovely because it is full of vowels, *which are all different.* It is even a more beautiful line than those where the repetition of the same vowels or the same consonants sometimes are so melodious."

It is clear that he had studied closely Milton's metrical effects, the pauses, which he greatly admired, and the bold substitution of trochees for iambuses, instancing especially the line,

Burnt after them to the bottomless pit.

But it may be questioned whether in the word bottomless the accent did not, in Milton's time, fall more on the second syllable; it seems as though it were a modern tendency in English to throw the accent back, in such words as cóntemplate, which was certainly in former times contémplate—indeed Tennyson himself used the word with that accent.

In such lines as

Ruining along the illimitable inane

Tennyson was, if not consciously imitating Milton, at least adopting Milton's metrical instinct.

For Wordsworth he had the deepest reverence, and for his work profound admiration, though he was by no means blind to his critical defects.

The two poets met several times, and it is interesting to note that on one occasion Tennyson complained that he could not fire Wordsworth's imagination even by a description of a tropical island all ablaze with scarlet flowers. It was this absence of fire which made Tennyson say once that he thought Wordsworth "thick-ankled," an admirably humorous and penetrating criticism. He used to complain of his want of artistic skill, and say that great as he was, he was too one-sided to be dramatic. In the poem, *Tintern Abbey*, which he greatly admired, he said that Wordsworth showed a want of literary instinct.

On the other hand he called him the greatest English poet since Milton, and said that his very best was the best in its way that had been sent out by the moderns.   He said once that the line,

> Whose dwelling is the light of setting suns,

was "almost the grandest in the English language, giving the sense of the abiding in the transient."

But what touched him most in Wordsworth was the high sense of consecration to the poetic vocation, and the depth of tenderness and mystery, uniting in the deep consciousness of the Divine.   "You must love Wordsworth," he once exclaimed, "ere he will seem worthy of your love."   And here it will be well to quote the majestic compliment paid by Wordsworth to Tennyson on the subject of one of his poems.   "Mr. Tennyson," said the old poet, "I have been endeavouring all my life to write a pastoral like your *Dora* and have not yet succeeded."

Byron, he used to confess, had been the strongest poetical influence of his early years.   He was dominated by him, he said, till he was seventeen, and then he put him aside altogether.   His "merits are on the surface." he said.   "He was not an

artist or a thinker or a creator in the highest sense;
but a strong personality and endlessly clever."

Yet at the same time he fully realised the debt
that literature owed to Byron in kindling the poetical spirit of the generation. "Byron and Shelley,"
he wrote to Spedding, "however mistaken they may
be, did yet give the world another heart and new
pulses—and so are we kept going."

For Shelley, however, his admiration was less
profound; and it is probable that the chilly and
visionary philosophy of Shelley made a deep sympathy between the two minds difficult. "There is
a great wind of words," he once said, "in a good
deal of Shelley, but as a writer of blank verse he
was perhaps the most skilful of the moderns." He
admired *Epipsychidion;* but he thought that there
was a certain *abandon* in many of the poems which
argued a want of poetical restraint. "Shelley's *Life
of Life,*" he once said, "is a flight where the poet
seems to go up *and burst.*"

It may be inferred that Keats attracted Tennyson
in early years from the influence traceable in *Timbuctoo;* and it is evident that the two had much
in common. There is the same gorgeous profusion
of ornament, the same lavish and almost riotous
imagination, the same power of amassing luxurious
detail. In Tennyson's early work it is clear that
he was tempted at times to sacrifice the scheme of
his poem to its accessories; and until he reached

the age of thirty he did not fully realise the primary
importance of structure, the necessity of subordin-
ating ornament to design.

But it was not only the luxuriance of detail which
attracted Tennyson in Keats; rather it was the
reverse; he realised fully the weakness of Keats,
the uncontrolled turbulence of inspiration from
which he was beginning to free himself in his later
work. "Keats," he said, "with his high spiritual
vision, would have been, if he had lived, the greatest
of us all (though his blank verse was poor), and
there is something magic and of the innermost soul
of poetry in almost everything which he wrote."
Tennyson said once to Mr. Aubrey de Vere, "Compare the heavy handling of my workmanship with
the exquisite lightness of touch of Keats."

For Burns he had a great admiration; he ranked
him higher than Shelley and said that he held him
to be "an immortal poet if ever there was one."

Mr. Aubrey de Vere tells a delightful story in
this connection. He had been talking to Tennyson about Burns, and the latter said, with great
emotion, "Read the exquisite songs of Burns—in
shape, each of them has the perfection of the berry;
in light the radiance of the dewdrop; you forget
for their sake those stupid things, his serious pieces."
Mr. de Vere met Wordsworth the same day, and
mentioned Burns; Wordsworth broke out into
vehement praises of Burns, as the great genius who

had brought Poetry back to Nature. He ended,
"Of course I refer to his serious efforts, such as the
Cottar's Saturday Night—those foolish little amatory
songs of his one has to forget." Mr. de Vere told
the two criticisms to Sir Henry Taylor the same
evening, and he replied, "Burns' exquisite songs
and Burns' serious efforts are to me alike tedious
and disagreeable reading."

Certain of Tennyson's scattered dicta on poetry
are memorable; of Ben Jonson he said, after
praising some of his lyrics, "To me he appears to
move in a wide sea of glue." Browning, who was
a close personal friend, was, as a poet, always a
problem to him. Tennyson said of him that he
had "a mighty intellect; he has plenty of music in
him, but he cannot get it out." He could not
understand the apparent neglect of form going
hand in hand with such prodigality of language and
such facility of execution. He admired Matthew
Arnold as a poet, and after reading *Literature and
Dogma*, somewhat unkindly sent a message to him,
"Tell him to give us no more of these prose things."

Mr. Swinburne he called "a reed through which
all things blow into music." He praised the
"liquid" character of Gray's writing, and admired
Collins and Campbell, though he objected to the
juxtaposition of sibilants in the former, and said
that he wrote "hissing" lines.

He knew something of Hebrew, and liked to

read the Psalms in the original. He said once of the Song of Solomon that in reality it was a most lovely, tender and delicate idyll, utterly different from the " coarsely painted, misrepresented, ununderstandable story given in the Bible translation."

He read a good deal of the Classics, principally Æschylus, Euripides and Homer; he was fond of the tragic fragments. Of Pindar he once said that he was "a sort of *Australian* poet—long tracts of gravel with immensely large nuggets embedded."

Of Latin writers he read Virgil, Lucretius, Catullus and Horace. He was fond of pointing out the music of Virgil's lines, quoting

> Dixit, et avertens rosea cervice refulsit,
> Ambrosiæque comæ divinum vertice odorem
> Spiravere, pedes vestis defluxit ad imos,
> Et vera incessu patuit dea. Ille ubi matrem
> Adgnovit, tali fugientem est voce secutus.

as giving a good specimen of his ear for pauses. In the poem written for the nineteenth centenary of Virgil's death, he praises his phrasing and his diction.

> All the chosen coin of fancy flashing out from many a golden phrase.

and

> All the charm of all the Muses often flowering in a lonely word.

But what seems most to have dwelt in his mind was the pathos of the poet :—

> Thou majestic in thy sadness at the doubtful doom of human kind.

Horace he says that he did not admire till he was thirty; and though he respected the perfection of finish that Horace exhibits, it may be doubted whether the elegant worldliness of the poet, his worship of expediency and the unromantic Present can ever have moved Tennyson very deeply; he even found the neatness of his metrical handling too precise; Horace's Sapphic stanza, he used to say, "is like a pig with its tail tightly curled."

For Catullus he had a deep and genuine love, though the grossness of some of the poems was inexplicable to him. "Catullus," he once said, "says that a poet's lines may be impure provided his life is pure. I don't agree with him; his verses fly much further than he does."

He read Dante, as I have said, and placed him among the immortals; he used to say that the origin of his own *Ulysses* was not the *Odyssey*, but a tradition preserved by Dante.

Though he rated Goethe very highly as an artist, he thought him an even better critic; and had a great opinion of his luminous wisdom; he used to say admiringly of Goethe that he was an excellent critic though he always tried to say the best he could about an author, adding, "Good critics are rarer than good authors." He had a particular admiration for the sound of German, its great sonorous words; but he confessed it to be untranslatable, and held that its music could not be rendered in English.

French he read, but not very sympathetically.
The sense of national enmity was probably strong
in Tennyson; and the vein of exaggeration so
natural to French heroic poetry grated on him.
He did not like the Alexandrine metre; but he
admired French lyrists, such as Béranger and
Sully-Prudhomme.   He thought some of Alfred de
Musset perfect.   " I consider him a greater artist
than Victor Hugo, but on smaller lines.   Victor
Hugo," he continued, "is an unequal genius, sometimes sublime; he reminds one that there is only
one step between the sublime and the ridiculous.
'Napoléon génait Dieu'—was there ever such an
expression?"

The above dicta are by no means exhaustive—
and it must be remembered that they were thrown
out in easy conversation, not presented as serious
criticism—but they tend to show that Tennyson
ranged far afield in his reading, and read with a keen
discriminating taste.   Occasionally he made a serious
critical mistake; he said once that he believed that
Rogers' smaller poems might last; and after reading *Festus* drew a remarkable comparison between
himself and Mr. Bailey, saying that while he was
himself a wren beating about a hedgerow, the author
of *Festus* was like an eagle soaring to the sun.
But even the best critics are liable to temporary
derangement; and it may be said, as a whole, that
Tennyson's judgments are both fair and forcible,

and show a notable capacity for appreciating high literature ; moreover, in dealing with Tennyson, one instinctively feels that he never spoke from a sense of duty, or from a desire to pose, or from anything but a sincere and genuine feeling—which gives these rugged opinions a value which the more polished statements of a less incorruptible critic may be held to lack.

CHAPTER IX

IT is possible to get a very clear notion of Tennyson's methods in writing for two reasons: he
was very regular in his habits of composition, and
he was not in the least reticent about his art. He
believed that he had developed slowly and said
once that *Poeta nascitur, non fit* was an erroneous
statement. It should run *Poeta nascitur, et fit.*
He added that he supposed he was nearer thirty
than twenty before he was anything of an artist;
at the same time he remarked, complacently
looking at his own *Juvenilia*, "It seems that I wrote
them all in perfect metre." This claim, however, it
will be remembered was directly contrary to the
opinion of so excellent a judge as S. T. Coleridge.

He said once that he found the choice of subjects
always difficult, and that the difficulty increased as
he grew older. At the same time the germ of
many of his poems lay dormant in his mind for
many years; when once embarked upon a poem he
wrote with great facility and speed. "I can
always write," he said, "when I can see my sub-

ject whole," and again, that when he once had
the subject and the framework of a poem the
actual writing cost him but little trouble. Thus
Guinevere was finished in a fortnight, *Enoch Arden*
in the same time; the line, "At Flores in the
Azores Sir Richard Grenville lay," was on his desk
for years and the ballad was finished in a day or
two. He used to say that he was never so well in
health as when engaged in the actual writing of a
poem. Tobacco was a necessity to him when thus
at work, and he was at his best, he said, while
smoking his first morning pipe after breakfast. At
the same time he could not force himself to work.
He believed like Coventry Patmore in the value of
infinite leisure for a poet, and though his poetry
was seldom out of his mind, and though he always
had some work in hand, yet there were long
periods of brooding when he did no actual writing.
"I cannot say," he once wrote to Lushington, "that
I have been what you professors call 'working' at
it, that indeed is not my way. I have my pipe and
the muse descends in the fume."

He had the habit of always trying to express any
sight that struck him in a few trenchant words ; many
of these impressions were never registered, and were
consequently lost, but the result was that he had an
extraordinary readiness in writing and an immense
wealth of simile and poetical illustration at his
command. It may, indeed, almost without exag-

geration, be said that the wonder is not that he
wrote so much, but that he did not write more ;
poetry was to him at once the serious business and
the highest pleasure of life ; he had, however, an
intense dislike to the manual labour of writing, and
it is probable that if this had not been the case he
would have written even more profusely.   Some
of his great poems were written without any
particular scheme.   Thus *In Memoriam* is not in
the least a coherent and articulate whole.   A
large number of the poems were written quite
independently, and it was not until he began to
review them and consider them in mass that the
idea of a great connected whole entered his mind.

He had written in 1833 a prose sketch of the
Arthurian legend long before he began to work on
the *Idylls*, a scheme which is interesting because it
shows how far more mystical his original conception
of the poems was than his later execution.   It seems
as though when he had once embarked upon the
Idylls his interest in the characters and the humanity of the poems carried him away ; and though
there is no doubt a semi-mystical allegory running
through the whole, yet the drama and the delineation of character had an increasing attraction for
him.   He had a great dislike to being tied down
to an exact and definite conception of his subject.
" Poetry," he said once, " is like shot-silk with many
glancing colours.   Every reader must find his own

K

interpretation according to his ability, and according to his sympathy with the poet."

He gave immense thought and care to the form of poetry; most of his lyrics, he used to say, owed their origin to single lines, which took definite shape in his mind, and in accordance with which the whole poem was evolved. Thus *The Charge of the Light Brigade* took its origin and derived its metrical scheme from the line, "some one had blundered," though in deference to criticism he omitted the line from certain versions, ultimately replacing it. Very early in life he said, " If I am to make any mark at all it must be by shortness," which seems to mean that his ambition was then to be a purely lyrical poet; though the conception was afterwards greatly modified.

There is a very interesting reminiscence by Mr. Aubrey de Vere which relates to Tennyson's conception of form. "One night," says Mr. de Vere, "after he had been reading aloud several of his poems, all of them short, he passed one of them to me and said, 'What is the matter with that poem?' I read it and answered, 'I see nothing to complain of.' He laid his fingers on two stanzas of it, the third and fifth, and said, 'Read it again.' After doing so I said, 'It has now more completeness and totality about it; but the two stanzas you cover are among its best.' 'No matter,' he said, 'they make the poem too *long-backed;* and they must go at

any sacrifice.'   'Every short poem,' he remarked,
'should have a definite shape like a curve, sometimes a single, sometimes a double one, assumed by
a severed tress *or the rind of an apple when flung on
the floor.'* "

This is among the most interesting of Tennyson's
critical dicta.   It reminds one of the story of Gray
who remorselessly cut out some of the most beautiful stanzas of the *Elegy* because he said that they
made too long a parenthesis.   But it is characteristic
of the highest kind of artist.   The inferior craftsman
is so enamoured of single lines and stanzas, that he
is capable of adding even unnecessary stanzas to a
poem, in order to dovetail in the image that he ad-
mires, without reference to the form of the poem.
Rossetti once said that the thing which made all the
difference between a good and a bad poem was the
"fundamental brain-work" involved in the former;
and ornament must be sternly sacrificed to construction if the workmanship is to be perfect.   Tennyson
himself said that a small vessel on fine lines is
better than a log raft.

How high a value he placed on style may be
inferred from the fact that he once said to Mr.
Gosse, "It matters very little *what* we say; it is
how we say it—though the fools don't know it."
He realised that the number of new thoughts that
a writer can originate must be small—if indeed it
is the province of a poet to originate thought at all

—and the vital presentment, the crystalline con-
centrations of ordinary experience is what he must
aim at.

With regard to metre he always said that blank
verse was by far the most diffcult form to write in.
He said once that the ten-syllabled line could
contain as few as three and as many as eight beats,
and that it was essential to vary the number of
beats to avoid monotony. He also held very strong
theories about the interchange of vowel sounds;
and believed that though for a definite effect the
same vowel sound might be repeated in close
juxtaposition, yet that the finest line contained
the largest possible variety of vowel sounds, suc-
ceeding each other in a melodious sequence. The
onomatopœic refrain, "lin-lan-lone," which was
invented as expressive of the sound of bells, is an
instance of this.

He held no less decided views about the juxtaposition of consonants : he had a particular aversion
to the recurrence of sibilants, making what he
called a "hissing" line. He used to say that he
never put two s—s together in his life.[1] The
getting rid of sibilants in a line he called in a
picturesque phrase, "kicking the geese out of the
boat."

He used to say with amusement that he was

[1] Though it is true that he once wrote in an album a poem
which contains the line, "Swift stars scud over sounding seas."

often accused of excessive alliteration, and that it was believed he used it deliberately. The case, as he once said, was the exact opposite. His tendency was to alliterate still more profusely than he did, and he was often forced to remove an excess of alliterated work.

He always held, as he says in his poem *To Virgil*, that the hexameter was the "stateliest" metre ever invented; but he did not think it fit for English; he once said that it was only fit for comic subjects—and he believed that Englishmen confused accent with quantity. He indicated that quantity had so little existence in English that for practical purposes it was superseded by accent, and that except for delicate effects, accent must be attended to; he always maintained that his experiments in classical metres had cost him more trouble than any of the poetry he had written.

It was strange that with his scorn of critics he yet altered so much. Probably no great poet ever rewrote so much in deference to criticism. Very different was the attitude of his great contemporary, Robert Browning, who when asked as to what omissions were to be made in a new edition of his poems answered briskly, "Leave out anything? certainly not!—*quod scripsi, scripsi.*" It is an instructive study to take Mr. Churton Collins' volume and compare carefully the various readings given in the footnotes. If one reads the early reviews of Tennyson's works one is struck with the unfamiliarity of many of the quotations; the reason is that it seldom happened that he did not alter almost everything to which critical objection was taken. One is further inclined to say unhesitatingly that he always altered for the better; but this belief depends largely upon the precise form in which one becomes acquainted with the poems. A modern student of Tennyson has delicious associations with so many lines, that the mere idea of substituting some of the earlier readings seems like a profanation; but possibly those who made the acquaintance of the poems in their earlier guise might think differently. Great poetry sinks so soon into the heart that the alteration of a word, even if the alteration is better from a literary point of view, is of the nature of a violent and blood-stained operation; it is impossible to judge poetry from the standpoint of severe literary judgment; much must be allowed for emotion; and one cannot make a greater mistake in reading and criticising poetry than not to allow for the natural influence of emotion and association.

There was a certain definite mood, if anything so intangible can be definite, which played a marked part in the early poetical life of Tennyson. This he called, "the Passion of the Past," and it is described with loving minuteness in a late poem, *The Ancient Sage*, which was confessedly autobiographical :—

To-day? but what of yesterday? for oft
On me, when boy, there came what then I called,
Who knew no books and no philosophies,
In my boy-phrase "the Passion of the Past."
The first grey streak of earliest summer-dawn,
The last long stripe of waning crimson gloom,
As if the late and early were but one—
A height, a broken grange, a grove, a flower
Had murmurs "Lost and gone and lost and gone !"
A breath, a whisper—some divine farewell—
Desolate sweetness—far and far away—
What had he loved, what had he lost, the boy?
I know not and I speak of what has been.

He once said in a letter to his future wife that the
far future had always been his world, and, as has
been mentioned before, his friend Spedding said of
him that he had an almost personal dislike of the
present whatever it might be.   But the mood, which
is the same as Virgil's "lacrimæ rerum," is not
merely the hunger of the sensitive spirit, which
finds life day by day overshadowed by some cloud
of subtle melancholy, and the imagined tranquillity
of existence fretted by the sorry and petty sting of
mundane cares.   It is rather the insistent pathos of
the world, the inevitable doom that waits for all
things, the pressure of mortality, the calling of
humanity out of the silent past, the cries of all
things *debita morti*, the delicious sadness which the
very transitoriness of mortal things evokes.   This
is the same mood as that described by William
Johnson, so pre-eminently the poet of youth :—

> But oh, the very reason why
> I love them, is because they die.

It was in this mood that two of the most soul-haunting lyrics of Tennyson's were written, *Break, break, break*, which was the work of an early morning in a Lincolnshire lane; and *Tears, idle Tears*, written at Tintern Abbey, and introduced into *The Princess;* of this Tennyson said that it was the expression not of real woe, but of the hungering melancholy of youth.

When the soul has had to bear the real sorrows of the world, and has trodden in the dark dry places, in which the suffering spirit walks, these experiences are apt to become, as it were, too tragic, too intense for expression. A grief seen very close is apt to freeze the sense of beauty at the very spring; and it is probably only in youth, before the heart has been seared by the dreary agonies of life, that such thoughts can be linked to sweetness at all. One who has suffered very deeply can minister, it may be, the consolation of faith and fortitude. The bereaved may dare to hope and look forward; but few hearts that have known the weight of sorrow can find a sense of luxurious melancholy in the thought of the "days that are no more."

As life went forward with Tennyson, and the thought of life, its possibilities and its failures, became more urgent, this rapture, the θεῖόν τι πάθος of which Plato spoke, became less and less possible.

Before the Franco-Prussian war he had written some little lyrics—*Window Songs*—which were set to music by Sullivan and published while the two great nations were engaged. Only the promise that he had made, and the knowledge of the loss and disappointment that would be caused by his refusal, induced Tennyson to allow the songs to be circulated. " I am sorry," he wrote, "that my four-year-old puppet should have to dance at all in the dark shadow of these days."

After the publication of *Maud*, in 1855, there seems a curious ebbing of the spring of inspiration. From that time dates a certain resolute search for poetical material, a certain husbanding of resources ; frequent inquiries among his friends for incidents and subjects—answered in the most conscientious and philosophical spirit by Jowett—while the old plenitude of fancy, the bubbling-over of the fountain of beauty was more rare. Edward FitzGerald maintained that after the 1842 volumes there was a perceptible decline in the work of the Poet ; indeed, though he veiled the thought in courteous periphrasis, it is clear that he thought Tennyson, either by reason of some warping of judgment, or by the desire to win popular favour, began to misuse his genius and trifle with it.

It is not necessary to go as far as Edward Fitz-Gerald in these matters, but there is a great deal of truth in what he said. Tennyson was indeed radically affected, not in a petty way, by his increased fame. The tremendous publicity of all he gave to the world overshadowed him. He became more shy of writing anything which could run counter to public taste or expectation, and, moreover, he felt impelled, by a certain conscientious sense of responsibility, based upon his theory of poetry, to keep in touch with popular movements, and to direct popular sentiment. In this way he undoubtedly increased the circle of his readers, and his influence upon thought was immensely augmented. But one misses the wild freshness of the earlier inspiration. It is impossible not to feel that the Poet is treading more warily, and though the result was undoubtedly an accumulation of poetical prestige, yet the clarity of his genius was somehow impaired. Leigh Hunt had written of one of the early volumes that he was fearful of what Tennyson would come to by reason of certain misgivings in his poetry and a want of the active poetic faith. This criticism was scarcely justified when it was made; but it is hard to say that it was not justified later on.

It is interesting here to note the view taken of Tennyson by the great French critic, Taine. He begins by saying that English men of sentiment had begun to weary of the Byronic school. "Men wanted to rest after so many efforts and so much excess." Tennyson, he says, stepped upon the stage at precisely the right moment. "His poetry was like lovely summer evenings: the outlines of the landscape are the same then as in the daytime; but the splendour of the dazzling vault is dulled."

He says that in the early poems there was too much voluptuousness, too great refinement: "He strayed through nature and history, with no pre-occupation, without fierce passion, bent on feeling and enjoying; culling from every place, from the flower-stand of the drawing-room and from the rustic hedgerow, the rare or wild flowers whose scent or beauty could charm or amuse him. Men entered into his pleasures; smelt the graceful bouquets which he knew so well how to put together; preferred those which he took from the country."

Twice or thrice, Taine thought, in *Locksley Hall* and *Maud*, Tennyson broke out into the passionate utterance which his tranquil and prosperous life tended to keep in the background. But he adds that, discouraged by criticism and by the be-wilderment which such poems caused to those who loved him for his rich serenity, he "left the storm-clouds and returned to the azure sky. He was right!"

Taine thought little of *In Memoriam*. He found a want of *abandon* in the elegy—a correct-ness, a restraint about the grief depicted, which seemed to him essentially unreal.

He draws an elaborate picture of the easy,

luxurious, sensible life of England; he describes the landscape: "If there is a slope, streams have ɔeen devised, with little islets in the valley, thickset with tufts of roses; ducks of select breed swim in the pools, where the water-lilies display their satin stars. Fat oxen lie in the grass, sheep as white as if freshly washed, all kinds of happy and model animals, fit to delight the eye of an amateur and a master." He ends by saying, "Such is this elegant and ɔommon-sense society, refined in comfort, regular in conduct, whose dilettante tastes and moral principles confine it within a sort of flowery border, and prevent it from having its attention diverted." Tennyson's poetry, he says, "seems made expressly for those wealthy, cultivated, free business men, heirs of the ancient nobility, new leaders of a new England. It is part of their luxury, as of their morality; it is an eloquent confirmation of their principles, and a precious article of their drawing-room furniture." He concludes by an elaborate comparison of Tennyson and Alfred de Musset; Tennyson the favourite poet of minds in which everything is rational and comfortable, where everything is taken for granted; De Musset the poet for a restless nation, certain of nothing, all alive to intellectual stimulus and new ideas—the poet of revolt.

This is an interesting judgment, because Taine has all through a scrupulous desire to do Tennyson justice; but the contempt which he felt at the bottom of his heart for a poet whose views he considered frankly *bourgeois* shows its head again and again, in a certain patrician insolence of tone, a consciousness that he is on the right side of the water after all.

CHAPTER X

THE true and devout Tennysonian will approach the earlier poems with a sacred reverence and a secret delight which the later works fail to command. As FitzGerald said in a beautiful letter, "Alfred, I see how pure, noble and holy your work is," and again he wrote: "When I look into Alfred's poems I am astonished at the *size* of the words and thoughts. Words so apt, full of strength, music and dignity."

It is perfectly true that the fame of Tennyson largely depends on the later works, *In Memoriam, Maud,* the *Idylls.* But these form as it were the pedestal on which the statue stands. The true Tennyson is the Tennyson of the early lyrics. I do not say that he did not at a later date produce poems which are worthy to stand with the earlier work. But I would unhesitatingly affirm that the two 1842 volumes are the consummate flower and crown of Tennyson's genius. It is not unfair to say that he attained a fame by work which was not his best, which he fully deserved for his best work.

We find Coventry Patmore writing: "Among Tennyson's works the second of the two little volumes published in 1842 contains, to my thinking, the greater part of all that is *essential* in his writings. It bears to them the same relation that Keats's little volume issued in 1820 does to all else he wrote. *In Memoriam* and *Maud* are poor poems, though they contain much exquisite poetry. Probably no modern work has done so much to undermine popular religion as *In Memoriam.* Tennyson's best work, though in its way a miracle of grace and finish, is never of quite the highest kind. It is not finished *from within.* Compare the finish of *Kubla Khan* with that of *The Palace of Art.*" This is a hard saying, but very subtle, and probably true, if we allow ourselves to adopt Patmore's rigid standpoint.

These first poems are to the rest of his writings what the first pale delicate foliage of spring is to the strong metallic leaf of summer. It may be affirmed that poets as a rule do their best work before their thirty-fifth year. About that age a man of even the highest genius becomes to a certain extent a materialist. The advantages of domestic comfort, of a stable income, of a definite place in the world become obvious. Matrimony, in the majority of cases, forces upon the mind the necessity for making a certain provision for wife and children; moreover the physical constitution loses its spring; chronic complaints begin to peep and beckon; the reserves of nervous force grow low; the painful brevity of human life becomes more obvious. The limitless possibilities of youth become conditioned by the actual. Moreover the social interest of life increases. Relationships, friendships, associations assert their claims. The rush and movement of the world, so aloof, so daunting in youth, begins to reveal its fascination. Idealism grows weak, or rather is apt to fail in the presence of the pressure of laws and averages and material conditions.

In youth this is not so; the world is like an opening rose; like a sea where each wave in the slow procession of experience falls and breaks with a shock of delicate surprises. The pure and ardent spirit begins to be aware that what seemed the truisms and abstractions of literature are real breathing and burning facts, and half persuades itself that no one can have felt them so poignantly, so exquisitely before.

Tennyson by his constitution and habits of life was able to keep this ardent feeling alive longer than most men—and being moreover a conscientious and absorbed worker he was able to give effect to recollected emotion longer than many poets. But, for all that, the earlier poems remain the true, authentic and living expression of his genius, written as the fancy bade him, and without any

consciousness of position or influence, or any sense
of duty towards the world which waited for his
utterance.

Moreover, though money was never a conscious
factor in Tennyson's scheme of life, yet the dignified
leisure, the easy hospitality which he loved cannot
be attained without money, indeed without a
large income. He himself, too, had felt the old
impulse of the full heart flag ; the power of feeding
hour by hour in the contemplation of nature die
away. " I am not so able as in old years to commune
alone with Nature," he wrote to his future wife
before their marriage.

It is not intended here to give any close or
detailed criticism of the earlier work. The poems
of which I now speak are those included in the
volumes of 1830, 1832 [1] and 1842.

The 1842 publication consisted of two volumes ;
the former was mainly occupied by selections from
the 1830 and the 1832 volume, largely, as a rule,
recast and altered, the second volume of 1842 was
composed of original poems.

The recasting of the earliest poems is in itself
a matter of the deepest interest. Mr. Churton
Collins has done invaluable work in his book, *The
Early poems of Alfred Lord Tennyson.* He gives
all the poems of the three publications, subjoin-
ing in each case the earlier forms ; and any one who

[1] This volume was published in 1832, and post-dated 1833.

L

wishes to penetrate the technical secrets of Tennyson's art, so far as they can be penetrated, should give this book the closest study.   Mr. Collins gives few and apposite comments and elucidations, and keeps the reader intent upon the study of the actual words of the author.   The volume opens the door, so to speak, into the poet's workshop, and not only shows what his later critical taste rejected, but illustrates his endless patience in correction.

In the 1830 volume appear most of the dreamy portraits of imaginary women in which the matter is nothing, the form everything.   Of these the exquisite *Claribel,* a mere word-melody, is the most haunting.   There are several songs, conceived in the Shakespearian manner, with an attempt to treat a descriptive subject whimsically and with melodious originality.   Such is *The Owl.*   But the best of these is the autumn *Song,* which came to him in the garden at Somersby :—

A Spirit haunts the year's last hours,

which is of indescribable beauty, personifying the spirit of the chill evening and the dying leaf,

To himself he talks ;
For at eventide, listening earnestly,
At his work you may hear him sob and sigh
In the walks.

Here, too, is the *Supposed Confessions,* an interesting autobiographical fragment, suppressed, after its first appearance, until 1871, when it was published in the *Juvenilia*, which is considered elsewhere.

Here, too, are the two poems *The Poet* and *The Poet's Mind*, which will be examined separately; some sonnets which were never reprinted, *The Ballad of Oriana* and the splendid *Ode to Memory*, which is probably the most typical of the early volume. It is written in an irregular odic metre, some of it reminiscent of the stately march of the *Lycidas*, but also containing some exquisitely original descriptive passages, such as

> the waterfall
> Which ever sounds and shines
> A pillar of white light upon the wall
> Of purple cliffs, aloof descried.

And again :—

> Long alleys falling down to twilight grots,
> Or opening upon level plots
> Of crowned lilies, standing near
> Purple-spiked lavender.

The scheme is loose, and the mood follows its wayward course : but the handling is masterly.

The general beat is iambic, with a few dactylic lines interspersed. I know few metrical openings so fine as that in the fourth stanza, when, the first strophe having come to an end, with a reversion to the original subject, the new strophe begins with the splendid line :—

> *Come forth, I charge thee, arise.*

The 1832 volume contains some far more mature work. Here are *The Lady of Shalott*, which was almost entirely recast in 1842, *Mariana in the South, The Miller's Daughter, Œnone* (practically rewritten in 1842), *The Palace of Art, The May Queen, The Lotos-Eaters* (much altered later), and *A Dream of Fair Women*—the very names have a potent magic as one writes them down.

Finally in 1842 appeared the *Morte d'Arthur, Love and Duty, Locksley Hall, Break, break, break*, perhaps one of the purest and least elaborate flashes of his genius; and many other poems of importance.

On the whole the 1832 volume is the most significant; the 1830 volume was one of immense promise, but had it stood alone, it could hardly have done more than creep into anthologies. The 1832 volume must have given Tennyson a place among English poets. The 1842 volume put him at the head of all living English poets, except Wordsworth, and profoundly affected the course of English literature.

What strikes any reader of these volumes is first the extraordinary variety of the fare provided. They do not show a point of view, they are no *tenuis vena*, a secluded garden-plot sedulously cultivated— but they are bold experiments in almost every kind of lyrical poetry.

There are poems of pure fancy dealing with those

elvish and aerial creatures that the old and childish dreams of man have originated and retained, spirits of flood and fell, fairies and mermen. There are English *genre* poems, such as *The Miller's Daughter* and *The May Queen*, capable of touching the simplest imaginations. Some have indeed contemned these poems as worthy only of being included in books of popular recitations; but to my mind few things show more clearly the simplicity of Tennyson's genius. No *précieux* writer, with a care for his reputation, could have dared to write them; and after all the deepest of all vulgarities is the studied avoidance of what may be thought to be vulgar.

Then there are autobiographical poems, ballads, sonnets, love-studies, satirical or philosophical pieces, like *The Vision of Sin*, which FitzGerald said touched on the limit of disgust without ever falling in, and, what are perhaps more distinctly Tennysonian than any other poems—a class which he may be held practically to have invented—are the pictorial poems such as *The Lady of Shalott* and more particularly the *Dream of Fair Women*, and *The Palace of Art*, which are really little galleries of pictures. All of them, as FitzGerald wrote, commenting on the trend of popular taste in the direction of greater elaborateness, "being clear to the bottom as well as beautiful do not seem to cockney eyes as deep as muddy water."

If one must indicate a fault in these poems it is

perhaps an excessive exuberance of detail, a profusion of richness which he learnt afterwards to avoid; but this is a *dulce vitium* after all. Tennyson said that he became an artist very slowly—and we are extraordinarily happy in possessing, so to speak, the very workshop before our eyes. The poems which he rewrote had failed, if they can be said to have failed, by a sort of delicious simpleness like the talk of a child. He was never afraid in these early days of simpleness—indeed the deliberate inclusion of such poems as the *O Darling Room*, and the retention of the *Skipping Rope*—poems of almost rich fatuity—show that he had a consistent view which was not affected by opinion. Of course there are cases in the poems when he falls into what may be called the "Early Victorian" vein—but these are mostly *genre* passages which when they have had time to grow quaint will be regarded affectionately as both minutely and deliciously characteristic of the social atmosphere of the time. Such stanzas are

> She left the novel half uncut
> Upon the rosewood shelf;
> She left the new piano shut:
> She could not please herself.
> (*The Talking Oak.*)

I print in an appendix the two most interesting of the rewritten poems, *The Lady of Shalott* and *The Palace of Art*, that the process may be studied at leisure[1]: it will be seen that the alterations invariably gain strength and weight without sacrificing simplicity; but there is nothing which to me gives a stronger impression of Tennyson's critical power than the various unpublished poems which his son has printed in the biography throughout the *Memoir*. The tact of the poet which withheld them from being incorporated with the great works was perfect; and may I add that the tact which dares to reproduce them now in the biography, where we are dealing with the making of a poet and not his finished work, is hardly less admirable.

Another characteristic which deserves a word in these earlier poems is the metrical richness which they display.

Tennyson was fond of a certain kind of informal metre, a mixture of dactyls, trochees, anapæsts and iambics, which he gradually deserted; his poems became more strict and regular as his artistic sense grew. But I believe that these irregular structures may have a great future before them. Mr. Swinburne seems to have practically exhausted the dactylic possibilities of English metres, and to have carried the length of lines to a degree that no one with a less absolute gift of melody could have

[1] By the kindness of Mr. Churton Collins I am permitted to print these poems from his edition of *The Early Poems of Alfred Lord Tennyson*, Methuen & Co., 1900, pp. 43 to 49 and pp. 86 to 100.

dared to do. But no one has yet developed the irregular scansions to which Tennyson devoted so many early experiments. There is no mere sloppiness of execution here, crowding syllables into a beat, so that it requires a kind of preliminary practice before they can be read ; but it is a perfectly deliberate irregularity. I give a few lines, mere word-music, from *The Sea-Fairies,* as it was published in 1830 :—

Whither away, whither away, whither away? Fly no more !
Whither away wi' the singing sail? whither away wi' the oar?
Whither away from the high green field and the happy blossom-
     ing shore?
  Weary mariners, hither away,
    One and all, one and all,
  Weary mariners, come and play ;
  We will sing to you all the day ;
    Furl the sail and the foam will fall
    From the prow ! one and all
    Furl the sail ! drop the oar !
      Leap ashore !
Know danger and trouble and toil no more.
Whither away wi' the sail and the oar?
        Drop the oar,
        Leap ashore,
        Fly no more !
Whither away wi' the sail? whither away wi' the oar?

This passage from the literary point of view has obvious faults with which I am not concerned, such as a certain feebleness of iteration. But I think that from a purely metrical point of view it is an astonishing performance. I would note the rapid choriambic beat slowing down, the exquisite pauses like a ticking wheel coming slowly to rest, quickening its pace, and dropping into rest again.

Indeed I have fancied that many of these experiments of Tennyson were suggested to him, not by musical time, but by the more irregular and natural beat of homely things. the ticking of clocks, the thud of oars in rowlocks, the clang and clink of hammers, the rolling of wheels, the purring of cats, the thin song of kettles, the drowsy hiccoughs of cisterns. All the world is full of rhythmical noises ; and the dreaming ear of Tennyson seems to have been peculiarly sensitive to such things.

CHAPTER XI

IT is impossible within the limits of this little book to give an exhaustive or detailed criticism of all Tennyson's works. I can but touch a few salient points and indicate a few characteristic pieces.

There is one pair of poems which it is obvious and natural to contrast, because the latter was written as a sequel to the former, *Locksley Hall* and *Locksley Hall Sixty Years after*.

The hero of the first *Locksley Hall* is a boy of twenty, an idealist who is sore and bruised by the envious contact of the world. His cousin whom he had loved as a child has been torn from him and "mated with a clown," whose only merit is that of superior wealth. The lover tells the unhappy story, and foresees the miserable slavery of the union; he thinks that the sorrow has killed the old visions within him, but as the poem advances he finds that the old enthusiasms still have power over him, and that he can still take a brave part in the march of the world.

(162)

The poem is full of *saeva indignatio*. The poverty
that in Tennyson's own case kept him from marriage
and the happy hearth lies heavily on him; he rages
against the "social wants that sin against the strength
of youth," and cries :—

Every gate is thronged with suitors, all the markets overflow.
I have but an angry fancy ; what is that which I should do ?

But over the whole poem broods an indescribable
light—the light of romance, mystery, call it what
you will; even Locksley Hall itself, with its wind-
swept gables overlooking the sand and the sea, has
that air of mystery and emotion that transfigures
the world.

The poem has faults; the language in places is
thin; the very metre halts. There is one line
which is absolutely unmetrical. Moreover there
are faults of taste; the theory of love that makes
the maiden pine in silent observance till rewarded
by the gift of a man's heart; the apparent arrogance
of such phrases as " *having known me*—to decline on
a range of lower feelings "—these are obvious
blemishes. But all is condoned—nay, the very
faults themselves become delectable—in the splendid sweep and passion of the poem, the purity of
the delineation of maternity, the gorgeous visions
of the future, the haunting melancholy of the
incidental touches.

It comes home to the reader of the poem that

beauty of expression was in the writer's mind throughout; even in the passion of intimate feeling there is room to turn aside to little touches of exquisite beauty that thrill the spirit with music; and at the end, where the future opens before the eye, there is little that is materialistic, little that is borrowed from the coarse current of practical life, while the emotion is not so far remote from life as not to be able to communicate something of its glow to material things. Not to multiply instances I would note particularly the splendid simile, which Tennyson took from a book of travels, which describes the slow thickening of revolutionary tendencies round an indolent and unconscious oligarchy :—

Slowly comes a hungry people, as a lion, creeping nigher,
Glares at one that nods and winks behind a slowly dying fire.

This is the truly poetical method of handling politics, and is by no means the only instance in the poem. Few indeed of Tennyson's poems have enriched life with such a treasury of stately phrase and exquisite music.

We turn to the second *Locksley Hall,* and somehow the glamour is gone; in *The Miller's Daughter,* long before, he had written words that were now to come sadly true :—

So, if I waste words now, in truth
You must blame Love. His early rage
Had force to make me rhyme in youth,
And makes me talk too much in age.

It is not that the old man has lost the passion of his youth, for he is infinitely more passionate; but where the young hero prophesied, the old man rants, where the younger comforted his despair by glowing hope and faith, the old man accentuates it by peevish railings and melodramatic fury. "I never scream," he had written to Spedding in 1834, "I leave that to your vivid men." The case is sadly altered now. Everything is poisonous, galling, roaring, raving. The whole world is plunged into vile and shameless sensuality, filthy selfishness, hopeless anarchy. The chariot has run away and the Master of created things sits in helpless apathy.

Even the domestic background is changed; the grandson has had a disappointment in love; but his Judith is a worldling born of worldlings; and the old man has nothing but the iciest contempt for what has moved his grandson's heart.

The poem in places falls into pits of mere prose; words and thoughts entirely alien to the spirit of poetry come whirling out. What could be more pitiful than such lines as these?

Set the maiden fancies wallowing in the troughs of Zolaism,

or

Poor old Heraldry, poor old History, poor old Poetry passing hence.

The whole poem, except for a few matchless lines that flash for an instant the old light upon the

tumultuous flood of rhetoric, is depressing, disquiet-
ing, even revolting. One cannot but be amazed at
the extraordinary vigour, the furious energy of the
old man, with his riotous disbelief in progress, his
wild and dreary impeachment of everything and
everybody; the workmanship of the poem is of
singular excellence as well. The late Lord Lytton
said that he admired the poem more as a work of
courage than as a work of art. Indeed the Poet
seems to have not only not lost in vigour, but to
have positively multiplied it—but what before was
tragic, dignified and pathetic courage, has now been
transmuted into insane, tempestuous, acrid violence.
One would have hoped to find a larger faith, a wider
sympathy, a more tranquil and clearer wisdom; but
all that age seems to have conferred is a deeper
cynicism and an increased vocabulary of vituperation.

It must be borne in mind that Tennyson was
working in a depressed mood, under the shadow of
a great bereavement; but it might have been hoped
that this would have made him lay loving hands on
the sorrows of the world, not chastise and belabour
it. The great sorrow of his life, the death of
Arthur Hallam, had never betrayed him into loss
of dignity.

We rise from the perusal of the second *Locksley
Hall* with astonishment at the intellectual vigour
and emotional violence of the old man, but with
neither veneration nor tenderness. The prophecies

ring hollow; they are the prophecies of one who has fed his mind in solitude on police reports, not of one who has gone in and out among the sorrowful and the glad. We wish that he could have been brave enough, if he felt as he did, to keep silence; he could hardly have hoped that his words would reach the ears of those whom he castigated, and the scourge is laid upon the backs of those who loved him best.

The poem of *Ulysses* demands a few words, not only because of the majestic simplicity of the poem, but because it shows the idealistic faculty of Tennyson at its height. The wise and high-hearted prince of Tennyson's poem has little except his restless and insatiable activity in common with the crafty and wary materialist of the *Odyssey*, with his preference for tortuous diplomacy. Any one who will read the *Odyssey* through in a candid spirit, will feel at the end that he has not been reading the life of a magnanimous or amiable man. He will not fail to admire the patient dexterity, the shrewd ability of the hero, and though his blood be set tingling by the spectacle of unconquerable courage, and by the stern completeness of his revenge, yet he will find little generosity or greatness in the character. He will rather feel he has been dealing with a consummate man of business. Ulysses in the twentieth century would not be a soldier or a statesman; he would rather make a large fortune in South African mines.

But Tennyson's Ulysses is an idealist, with an intense and burning curiosity, a high adventurousness. It is the same transfiguring change that in the ballad of *The Revenge* made a courteous and high-minded hero out of a very tough and unscrupulous old sea-dog.

But we need not quarrel with the poem on this account. It has none of the subtle analysis which Browning would have bestowed upon a character-sketch, but it is great in conception and greater still in execution. The weariness of the settled life, the contemptuous wonder at the torpid content with which he is surrounded, come first—then there is the description, grave and affectionate, of the sober-minded son whose dutiful horizon is so tranquilly limited—and here mingles a certain shade of impatience at the contrast. Then the old ardour springs up, the thirst to steer again into the unknown, and the poem rises, strong and noble to the matchless close, celebrating the joys of endurance, the glory of going on.

Tennyson's *In Memoriam* is probably the noblest monument ever raised by the human spirit to the memory of a lost and unforgotten friend. Moreover it commemorates the highest and holiest form, because the purest, of human relationship—an equal friendship. Into such a passion flow all the best and brightest streams of life, the dreams of ardent manhood, the rapt surprises of the opening mind, the generous hopes of youth, absolutely untainted by anything that can lower or enervate. So many able analyses have been made of this complex work that it is only necessary to indicate its scope. It is the story of an overwhelming loss, when a soul is confronted by the fact that a kindred spirit, to whose touch all the chords of the survivor's being had vibrated, is suddenly swept, without a shadow of warning, a hint of doom, into the unseen; and the bereaved stretches feeble hands into the darkness, and finds no answer there; such a loss freezes the heart at the very source; very gradually the cloud lifts; the healing influence of time asserts itself; and the grieving spirit rises out of the shadow into a firm belief in immortality and into an absolute trust in the great purpose of God.

The poem was not precisely planned. It had no conscious scheme; it is rather a garden of a sorrowing spirit, set with rue and rosemary, and other fragrant herbs of remembrance and regret, than a single tree, branching into sombre shade from a single stem. The mistake has often been made of considering it to be a poem with a definite inception and a precise form. Tennyson himself said otherwise; it was not till many of the poems had been written, *à plusieurs reprises*, that it occurred to him that it would form a connected whole. Then he bridged a few gaps, put in certain connecting links, and welded it together. But even

M

so the poem has no definite progression; it ebbs
and flows; it sometimes pursues a single thought
minutely, apart from the general scope of the
poem, sometimes takes up a previous thought and
enlarges it.

His own view of the poem seems to have varied
with his mood; if the passion of the poem was
accused of being imaginary, artificially stimulated,
impossibly deep, he would say, "I have written
what I have felt and known, and I never will write
anything else." But if on the other hand it was
attempted to attach what he considered too literal
a sense to any of the stanzas, to identify scenes or
persons too closely, he would say, "The mistake
that people make is that they think the poet's
poems are a kind of catalogue *raisonné* of his very
own self and of all the facts of his life." The two
attitudes are not inconsistent.

The metre had been used before by Ben Jonson,
Lord Herbert of Cherbury and others; but it was
new to Tennyson, and he was long under the impression that he had invented it. The form of the
stanza is peculiarly adapted for reflective and
aphoristic verse. It is the common long metre,
with the second pair of rhymes inverted, so as to
make each stanza complete, like a tree beside a
still water, with its reflection at its foot.

Tennyson gave the stanza so individual a stamp
that it is one of the easiest metres to imitate, with

its emphatic fourth line rounding the stanze off.
Indeed so entirely did he set his mark upo ı the
metre that it is almost a forbidden one for poets,
because of the almost hopeless impossibi ity of
writing it except in the Tennysonian manner.

The thought is generally lucid ; but the language
is in places highly obscure, from the com ression
exercised.

If the entire poem is read swiftly, as it deserves
to be, at a sitting, besides being studied minutely,
the fact which strikes the reader, which may otherwise escape him, is the large number of abs lutely
unemphatic poems [1]—poems which though of perfect
workmanship and unexceptionable sweetness, seem
to add nothing to the progress of the thought, and
indeed leave no definite impression upon the mind.   I
venture to believe that these poems are in most cases
the connecting links which were afterwards inserted.

Moreover there are a considerable number of
poems [2] which contain, generally at the end, the
purest grain of gold ; these poems appear to have
been constructed to lead up to this climax, and the
effect of the concentrated close is perhaps heightened by the lucid simplicity of the lines which the
thought closes as with a clinching hammer-stroke ;
occasionally [3] the climax is reached before the e ıd,
and the finale is unemphatic ; but this is rare.

[1] *See* xviii., xlvi., lxii., xcii.
[2] *See* xxiv., xxxv., lxxv., cxvii.   [3] *See* iv., lxxxiii.

Tennyson had what we may call the Emersonian
faculty of producing a familiar thought and by
exquisite and curious phraseology bringing it home
to a reader's mind with a glow of perceptive and
original satisfaction.   Indeed it may be said that
the more familiar the thought is, the more it is part
of the common and vague stock of the reflective
mind, the more complete is the triumph.   A great
poet has no call to be fantastic, or to search for
thoughts that are out of the ordinary reach.   It is
for him to take a typical thought and crystallise
it—or, better still, to seize upon some half-formed
tendency of thought, such as is apt to haunt, with a
cyclic, almost epidemic contagion the minds of
men in a particular generation, and place it in a
definite light, and in a form when it becomes a
current token instead of a mere lingering, bright-
ening vision.   Such a couplet as

> 'Tis better to have loved and lost
> Than never to have loved at all—

is a supreme instance of this power.   Such a
thought is not new; but instead of being a vague
force it becomes, so to speak, a definite weapon,
with penetrative power that will hang, till superseded, in the armoury of thought.

Much has been said about the Christian teaching
of *In Memoriam*.   Tennyson himself used to say
when he was questioned about his Christian belief

that his answer was, "You will find it in *In Memoriam*, where I have written it."

It is interesting to find Coventry Patmore writing from Ambleside in August, 1850 :—

"Yesterday it was too wet to go to church, and Tennyson read prayers, lessons and a sermon by Maurice.

"The more I talk with him the more I discover that I was right in thinking that he has given a defective notion of his faith in *In Memoriam*. He is far above all the pantheistic 'religious faculty' humbug that taints so many half-geniuses in this day; and I am sure that he would be horrified if he knew that any such men had been led by *In Memoriam* to count him as a fellow-heathen."—C. P.

With every wish to find a definite Christian faith expressed in *In Memoriam* I must confess that I cannot certainly discover it there, though the poem is of course instinct with strong Christian feeling throughout.

The allusions to Christianity in the poem are the following :—

The prelude, beginning, "Strong Son of God, immortal Love," has been held by many to be a definite confession of faith in our Lord Jesus Christ. It seems to me that this cannot be maintained. I believe it to be an address, in which Christian phraseology is deliberately employed, to the principle of Divine Love; it appears to me that the words, "Thou madest Death," cannot be intended to be applied to the Redeemer; and I cannot help feeling that the phrases—

Our little systems have their day;

.   .   .   .

They are but broken lights of Thee—

are meant to include Christianity with other religious systems. There is nothing, I think, to justify the idea that Tennyson felt Christianity to be the final revelation made to man. If this poem stood alone I think it might be maintained that it was a confession of faith; but I believe that taking it in conjunction with other poems Tennyson made it doubtful on purpose, and left it ambiguous, not because he wanted to pose as a more definite Christian than he was, but because he had the deepest sympathy with the Christian spirit, and had no intention of alienating Christian readers by stating what I believe to be the fact, that he looked behind and beyond the Christian scheme of dogma for his own faith.

I say that if the poem stood alone the question would be difficult to decide; but considering the other allusions to Christianity in *In Memoriam* I think it is clear that though he approached his subject with a passionate faith in God, and the deepest religious feeling, that faith cannot definitely be called a Christian faith, except in the way that rationalists would define Christianity, as a revelation of God, without a historical basis.

Passing on we find in "xxxi." a poem devoted to Lazarus; this again does not, I think, amount to a definite confession of faith, but is introduced rather by way of illustration, to indicate with telling force the silence of the grave.   It will be noticed that no argument is built upon the miracle ; only the mystery is indicated that one who is recorded to have returned through the gate of Death had no tale of his experience to tell.

The following poem, "xxxii.," speaks of the faith of Mary—but the faith is spoken of merely from Mary's point of view.

In the following poem, "xxxiii.," the Poet speaks in a way which I am forced to believe is autobiographical.   And this poem is so vital to my argument that I give it in full :—

> O thou that after toil and storm
>   Mayst seem to have reach'd a purer air,
>   Whose faith has centre everywhere,
> Nor cares to fix itself to form,
>
> Leave thou thy sister when she prays,
>   Her early Heaven, her happy views ;
>   Nor thou with shadow'd hint confuse
> A life that leads melodious days.
>
> Her faith thro' form is pure as thine,
>   Her hands are quicker unto good :
>   Oh, sacred be the flesh and blood
> To which she links a truth divine !
>
> See thou, that countest reason ripe
>   In holding by the law within,
>   Thou fail not in a world of sin,
> And ev'n for want of such a type.

It seems to me clear beyond demonstration that the Poet addresses himself, that he places himself among those who do not care to fix their faith to form, and outside of those who link a truth divine to flesh and blood.

In " xxxvi." there is a definite allusion to Christian faith :—

> And so the Word had breath, and wrought
>   With human hands the creed of creeds
>   In loveliness of perfect deeds,
> More strong than all poetic thought.

But this confession loses rather than gains in force from being the expansion of the thought in the previous stanza that

> Truth *embodied in a tale*
> Shall enter in at lowly doors.

In the following poem, " xxxvii.," comes a dialogue between *Urania* the Muse of Religion, and *Melpomene* the lyric Muse, where *Urania* chides *Melpomene* for meddling with sacred mysteries. *Melpomene* speaks for the Poet and claims to be but an earthly muse, brooding over the thought of the dead friend, and while she deprecates censure claims to be allowed to touch the skirts of faith.

> I murmur'd, as I came along,
>   Of comfort clasp'd in truth reveal'd ;
>   And loiter'd in the master's field,
> And darken'd sanctities with song.

But that the Poet claims his share in the divine example of Christ is shown by " lii.," where the spirit of true love speaks :—

What keeps a spirit wholly true
  To that ideal which he bears ?
  What record ? not the sinless years
That breathed beneath the Syrian blue :

So fret not, like an idle girl,
  That life is dashed with flecks of sin.

This is a large and tolerant philosophy, but it is conceived more in the spirit of Christ than in the spirit of dogmatic Christianity.

In "lxxxiv." is a stanza which would seem to amount to a confession of the Divinity of Christ ; and here indeed I find it hard to understand how it was written except with the deliberate intention of keeping within the fold. He speaks of the meeting with his friend after death, and how the two souls together should

Arrive at last the blessed goal,
  And He that died in Holy Land
  Would reach us out the shining hand,
And take us as a single soul.

But then again " cvi.," the lyric of the Christmas Bells, where he speaks of those bells ringing in " the Christ that is to be," seems to point to the poet's belief in some far-off expansion, or even reconstitution of the Christian revelation.

But one point seems to me to be absolutely conclusive. There is no allusion in the whole poem to the Resurrection, the cardinal belief of Christianity, the very foundation-stone of Christian belief; the very essence of consolation, of triumph over death, of final victory. It is impossible that one who was a Christian in the strictest sense should not have recurred again and again to this thought in a poem which deals from first to last with death and hope. And this seems to me to outweigh all positive testimony; if the Resurrection had been part of the vital faith of the Poet, it must have been the very crown and sum of his sorrowing hopes; but if it was to him rather a hope than a belief, then I cannot think that *In Memoriam* alone entitles him to be called, in the ordinary acceptance of the word, a Christian poet.

But it is doubtless as well that a poet should not hold too closely to the exact orthodox position of the day. The so-called orthodox position is seldom precisely the same for ten years together. When Cowper, in a fine burst of indignation, wrote :—

> Drill and bore
> The solid earth, and from the strata there
> Extract a register from which we learn
> That He, who made it, and revealed its date
> To Moses, was mistaken in its age—

he wrote what no doubt confirmed many a timid heart, and gave a glow of comfortable conviction to many a pious soul, that geology after all was hopelessly misleading, compared with the book of Genesis, as to the antiquity of the earth.

It was not unnatural that Cowper should feel as

he did, and so feeling should write as he did. But we see that he was meddling with matters he had better have left alone, and that the duty of the poet is not to take a hand in theological controversy, but to clarify motive, to touch principles with emotion, and to provide human nature with a more generous guide than either orthodoxy or rationalism.

Tennyson certainly thought that the teaching of Christ had fallen far too much into Pharisaic hands. He said in *Maud* that

> The churchmen fain would kill their church
> As the churches have killed their Christ,

and while he burned to see religion left confidently in the possession of simple-hearted men, he was equally anxious not to assail its dominance, not to be, as he wrote in his address to the Queen in 1872, a

> Fierce or careless loosener of the faith.

CHAPTER XII

*T*HE *PRINCESS* is not one of Tennyson's greatest works, though it contains many passages and lines of extraordinary and memorable beauty; indeed some of the incidental lyrics "imbedded and injellied" in it are among the best of Tennyson's work.

He had no great opinion of the poem himself; the sub-title, *A Medley,* is indeed intended to serve as a shield against the critics—and the ruthless way in which the unities are disregarded shows that the Poet did not intend the poem to be taken seriously *per se,* though the principle indicated in it is serious enough. The most elementary historical conventions are set at defiance. The Prince and his knights fight in armour, with sword and lance, while the court physician poises a gilt-headed cane and talks of catalepsy. The historical allusions in the discourses of the Princess and her lecturesses are somewhat sedulously drawn as a rule from ancient instances; but the Lady Psyche talks of Elizabeth and Bacon, and mentions "Kaffirs,

Hottentots, Malays." The Princess herself is learned in nineteenth-century astronomy and geology; she is acquainted with the nebular hypothesis, rides on a mutual-improvement picnic, "to take the dip of certain strata to the North." She abhors vivisection; and her girl-graduates

> chatter stony names
> Of shale and hornblende, rag and trap and tuff,
> Amygdaloid and trachyte.

This, however, matters little; Tennyson's aim was to place the theory of women's education in a romantic setting. The impression could not have been conveyed if the studies of these damsels had been confined to such science as existed in the days of chivalry; and on the other hand the romance of the poem could hardly have been sustained had the combats been fought with Maxim guns and Martini rifles.

Tennyson's theory of female education was a simple one, as his theories were. His maxim was that "either sex alone is half itself." His view is that marriage is better for the man and best for the woman; in the case of the latter, culture is only valuable in so far as it fits her for marital relations. He did not face the fact that under modern conditions there must be an increasing number of unwedded women; he would have said bluntly that they must try to get married without sacrificing maidenly delicacy, or at any rate fit themselves for

possible matrimony. The poem contains no gospel
for the *virgo debita virginitati*—nor indeed for
male celibates either; the Prince declares that the
loveless life for men is

> A drowning life, besotted in sweet self,

and that a man who loves not, either

> Pines in sad experience worse than death,
> Or keeps his wing'd affections clipt with crime.

The result is that the poem is lacking in dramatic
interest; there is no character on whom the interest
centres. The Prince himself is a haunted amiable
boy, whose knightly attributes do not carry conviction; and when he had secured Ida's love he
lectures her in a strain that hardly even passion
fortified by contrition could have tolerated:—

> "Blame not thyself too much," I said,

and

> dearer thou for faults
> Lived over.

The Prince in his bed-pulpit, initiating her into his
superior nobility of spirit, makes no attempt to
overlook or to throw into the shadow the faults of
her ideal. And when poor Ida says, "You cannot
love me," he declares with solemn condescension
that not only is it possible, but that even he from
his serene height of perfection can anticipate distinct
benefits to himself from their union.

The other characters, except Cyril and Gama, are but puppet-shapes; yet, though there is a want of dramatic unity, there are many dramatic scenes and episodes; such is the Lady Psyche recovering her lost child; such is the speech of Ida, where with a sublimity of scorn she thanks the Prince for the havoc he has made :—

> " You have done well and like a gentleman,
> And like a prince : you have our thanks for all :
> And you look well too in your woman's dress :"

the bitter self-restraint of the mood is well maintained, until at last the passion bursts all bounds and breaks out into majestic rage.

Moreover the whole poem from beginning to end is a mine of beautiful images, exquisite pictures, delicate thoughts and admirable lines. The technical workmanship is beyond praise, and yet the speeches as a rule are complicated and obscure. This is characteristic of Tennyson throughout; the lucid simplicity of his descriptive and lyrical passages with their admirable elaboration of detail gives place in his dialogue to an over-elaboration of language, and to a complexity of thought which makes the sense difficult to follow, and forfeits dramatic interest. It is strange that the charge of obscurity so frequently launched against Robert Browning has never been hinted against Tennyson; and yet I declare that the speeches, both in *The Princess* and the *Idylls*, are some of the most obscure reading that it is possible to discover in modern poetry—a strong desire for compression, for ornateness, for coagulating a clause into an epithet, for epigrammatic and proverbial touches making the language like a labyrinth of sonorous walls, even when the thought to be expressed is neither abstruse nor complicated.

> If indeed there haunt
> About the moulder'd lodges of the Past
> So sweet a voice and vague, fatal to men,
> Well needs it we should cram our ears with wool
> And so pace by : but thine are fancies hatch'd
> In silken-folded idleness ; nor is it
> Wiser to weep a true occasion lost,
> But trim our sails, and let old bygones be,
> While down the streams that float us each and all
> To the issue, goes, like glittering bergs of ice,
> Throne after throne, and molten on the waste
> Becomes a cloud : for all things serve their time
> Toward that great year of equal mights and rights,
> Nor would I fight with iron laws, in the end
> Found golden : let the past be past ; let be
> Their cancell'd Babels : though the rough kex break
> The starr'd mosaic, and the beard-blown goat
> Hang on the shaft, and the wild fig-tree split
> Their monstrous idols, care not while we hear
> A trumpet in the distance pealing news
> Of better, and Hope, a poising eagle, burns
> Above the unrisen morrow.

The descriptive passages, on the other hand, in the poem are among Tennyson's best work; we cannot fail to admire the art by which in a few gorgeous lines he brings the stately palace before us with its towers and corridors, its fountain-sprinkled

lawns, its bowery thickets. No poet can raise so
magic a vision of stately splendour, or suggest such
wealth of detail by an apposite instance as Tennyson.
The great glimmering palace, when at the end the
wounded warriors are being nursed back to life,
rises before us in its solemn silence, its cool and
echoing majesty. Outside, the moonlight sleeps
on the turf, thickens the twilight of the arched
walks and dim groves, where the milk-white
peacock droops like a ghost, while the fountain
drips and rustles in its marble pool. Slowly the
night deepens and pales towards the dawn. The
morning comes freshly and serenely in

> Till notice of a change in the dark world
> Was lispt about the acacias, and a bird,
> That early woke to feed her little ones,
> Sent from a dewy breast a cry for light.

It is in such pictures as these that Tennyson shows
his art; it is like the wave of a wand, and a magic
drawn from the depths of the forest, out of the
secret valleys of the mountain, is spread over the
senses like a cloud, and we are not what we were.

Tennyson's conception of woman is a very definite one: she is emphatically *the weaker vessel;*
he creates no exalted type of womanhood; he is
deeply sensitive of her beauty and purity, and the
reverence due to her; but it is to him an essential
thing in the perfect woman that, once wed, she
should be absolutely loyal and devoted, entirely

N

forgiving and unquestioning. Thus Geraint's treatment of Enid is abominable; what can be thought of the conduct of one who can break from passionate love into something very like brutality, without a single question asked, a single explanation attempted? Enid, indeed, hardly preserves her dignity. Again there is too much evidence that the Tennysonian lover watches his mistress and notes the signs of the devotion with which he inspires her, finally rewarding her in a princely manner with the gift of his love. There is little trace of the passionate and anxious wooing of the lover, the consciousness of the stainless purity which he can hardly hope or dare to call his own.

There is the love, for instance, of Elaine for Lancelot; there is the lover of *Locksley Hall*, who writes of his Amy :—

And her eye on all my motions with a mute observance hung.

There is the Lord of Burleigh who says in a royal manner :—

"Maiden, thou hast loved me well."

There is Edward Gray who reflects not with complacency indeed, but with no sense of unworthiness that

Ellen Adair was dying for me.

When Tennyson does make a stately figure like the Princess, who tries to be independent of the lords of creation, she is not to be gently wooed from her isolation, but sharply brought to her senses.

Even in *Maud*, where he comes most closely to the desperate humility of the lover, there is a good deal of bitter contempt for the view of Maud's brother that a morbid and poverty-stricken squire is not to be regarded as a particularly eligible suitor for one so richly dowered.

It must be confessed that Tennyson's view was, if not primitive, at least old-fashioned. He had no real belief in the equality of the sexes. Coventry Patmore is a far more advanced exponent of the faith of the devout lover; and though he too had a strong idea of wifely subjection in marriage, yet in the wooing time the mistress is a far more remote and ethereal creature, tremblingly desired and timidly demanded, a goddess to be tempted if possible from her chaste solitudes to be the guiding star of world-stained man.

Maud was received with much hostile criticism, and Tennyson used to complain that unintelligent readers persisted in considering it to be autobiographical, whereas he himself called it "a little Hamlet."

It is technically one of the most perfect of Tennyson's great poems. He had his instrument entirely under his command, and there is no poem which makes a reader feel more strongly that he produced exactly the effects he intended to produce.

He rides in the chariot and is not dragged behind it.

On the other hand it illustrates I think the beginning of the decadence of Tennyson's art, the dying away of the divinest impulses of pure beauty, the period at which the purely poetical impulse began to flag, and required to be roused by a violent situation, a tragic interest. The poem is full of stern anger, a Carlylean impulse to find fault, to deal heavy blows, to pierce and shatter.

We are introduced to a morbid young man, treading perilously near the confines of madness, with a ruined inheritance, which spurs the speaker to venomous diatribes on the subject of rotten commercial morality. For a time this is suspended in the exquisite surprise of the growing passion, which reaches its climax in the unsurpassable lyric, *Come into the garden, Maud,* where the pulse of the lover thrills and throbs through all created things, the hurrying streamlet, and the passionate expectation of the garden, through the fragrant dusk. Then comes the catastrophe; and the political indignation gathers head again in the great warlyrics at the end, which expand the thought of the social corruption indicated in the preliminary lyrics.

In spite of the nobility of much of the satire, in spite of the fact that all human interests and passion are the property of the poet, we may be allowed to wonder regretfully whether the bard is in his place pacing up and down the platform, and indulging in strident tirades against the general moral slothfulness of the world. Such exhortations do not issue very appropriately from the secluded haunts of the muse. FitzGerald said of Carlyle that he sate pretty comfortably in his study at Chelsea, scolding all the world for not being heroic, and not very precise in telling them how to be. It is the old story over again of the clergyman lecturing the dutiful persons who attended his ministrations on the heinous crime of absenting themselves. One ' wonders whether such diatribes ever reach the right ears; whether any "broad-rimmed hawker of holy things," or "smooth-faced snub-nosed rogue" ever felt a touch of honest shame at being thus held up to the contempt of literary people. One is irresistibly reminded of the gentleman in Mr. Mallock's *New Republic* who confessed that he did not care two straws about Liberty, but that his mind was often set all aglow by a good ode about her.

One feels with some pain that the dreamful youths, the enthusiastic maidens, who are the poet's most sympathetic audience, probably only derived a sharper sensation from the splendid rush of these vituperative and militant rhymes. There is a fable of some forgotten Poet Laureate being set to translate the war-songs of Tyrtæus to stir the martial hearts of English soldiers; the story goes that the ardent strains were read aloud in a barrack-room by a major-general who only desisted when he found the majority of his audience were wrapped in sleep.

We feel that perhaps the poet is better employed when he directly serves and touches the hearts that are alive to a craving for the beautiful; when he interprets the gentle secrets of the kindly earth and the generous heart, to minds thrilling with the vague sense of wonder and delight. To see beauty in simple events and homely things is the real work of the poet. It was otherwise perhaps when a nation was all intellectually alive like the Athenians, and when eager impulse was on the look-out for impassioned rhetoric. But now and here, though we may be grateful to Tennyson for his

> Sonorous metal, blowing martial sounds,

our gratitude is bound to be rather of the literary order than the ethical. In fact the poet must convince and caress, not denounce and storm.

The germ of *Maud* is the poem that stands fourth in the second part. This magnificent lyric, of irregular metre and informal scheme,

> Oh that 'twere possible,

was sent as has been related at the request of Lord Houghton in the year 1837 as a contribution to a sort of literary benefit—a little volume of miscellanies sold to assist a distressed literary man.

The poem is well worth study from the metrical point of view. Its scheme is a double beat, occasion-

ally increased.   It is a good instance of a poem
loosely constructed in a simple species of time,
without great exactness.

A friend of Tennyson's suggested that it wanted
expansion and elucidation ; and the lovely fragment
was expanded into the beautiful if intemperate
rhapsodical monodrama.

Maud was a poem of which Tennyson himself
was particularly fond.   There was none which he
read aloud more frequently, or rather chanted, in
the great deep musical voice.   It is full of original
metres, and Tennyson never displayed on such a
scale his extraordinary power of handling both long
and short rhythms.   The long metres are magnifi-
cently full and sonorous, and never drag.   But the
skill is even more delicately displayed in the short
metres with frequently recurring lines, where the
danger is of becoming choppy, so to speak, and
jerky, but which are models of delicate grace.

The general run of the poem is dactylic, but
irregular dactylic : that is to say the trochee is
frequently substituted for the dactyl.

I would quote as perhaps the most perfect and
characteristic example the poem which stands third
in the first part :—

Cold and clear-cut face, why come you so cruelly meek,
Breaking a slumber in which all spleenful folly was drown d,
Pale with the golden beam of an eyelash dead on the cheek,
Passionless, pale, cold face, star-sweet on a gloom profound ;

Woman-like, taking revenge too deep for a transient wrong
Done but in thought to your beauty, and ever as pale as before
Growing and fading and growing upon me without a sound,
Luminous, gemlike, ghostlike, deathlike, half the night long
Growing and fading and growing, till I could bear it no more,
But arose, and all by myself in my own dark garden ground,
Listening now to the tide in its broad-flung shipwrecking roar,
Now to the scream of a madden'd beach dragg'd down by the
    wave,
Walk'd in a wintry wind by a ghastly glimmer, and found
The shining daffodil dead, and Orion low in his grave.

It will be observed that the metre is one of beats and not of strict metrical feet. But quite apart from the melody of the lines I would instance the perfect structure of the poem, its inimitable " curve," as Tennyson would have said. And, as imitative verse, the penultimate lines describing the harsh chatter of the shingle, as the wave ebbs back, are surely unequalled. Nor less admirable is the quiet close, the rounding of the vignette by the sight of the dead flower and the sinking star.

I may perhaps say a few words about one particular idyll which seems to me to be highly characteristic of Tennyson. This is *The Brook*, which appeared first in the 1855 volume. The soliloquist is a man revisiting the scenes of his youth, but in a mellow and gentle frame of mind, with no sharp sense of loss. He speaks of a friend, a poet, whom he lost long ago, and quotes a few opening stanzas of a lyric, which gives its name to the idyll, and is afterwards inwoven in little snatches with the narrative.

The idyll itself is full of delicious lines, such as
the comparison of an old, lean, talkative farmer to
the

dry
High-elbow'd grigs that leap in summer grass.

The story is simple enough, a trickle of gentle reminiscence.   But the lyric itself is of rare beauty,
with its prattling refrain.

It may be interesting to observe that in one highly
characteristic and picturesque couplet,

With many a silvery waterbreak
Above the golden gravel,

the word which we should at once lay a finger on as
Tennysonian, "waterbreak," is one that he took from
Wordsworth.

But the whole poem is one that brings tranquillity
into the mind, like a pastoral landscape seen from
the windows of a train, all lit with golden summer
light ; while the lyric itself is in the very spirit of an
English streamlet, that sings its light-hearted song
all day among quiet fields.

The dialect poems too demand one word.   Tennyson was always interested and delighted with characteristic stories of country persons, true sons of the
soil.   These *genre* pieces illustrate in a remarkable
degree the richness and authenticity of Tennyson's
humour.   Poems of rustic life written by people of
another class have as a rule a fatal unreality about
them : but Tennyson partly from heredity, partly

from experience, and partly from art, is always con-
vincingly and pungently real.   The dialect itself
proves how strong was the art of mimicry for which
he was famed in earlier years.

FitzGerald wrote a delightful note about the
Northern Farmer: "The old brute," he says,
"invested by you with the solemn humour of
Humanity, like Shakespeare's Shallow, becomes a
more pathetic phenomenon than the knights who
revisit the world in your other verse."

CHAPTER XIII

THE *Idylls of the King* were regarded in Tennyson's lifetime as his great work, and probably will for some time be so regarded by his less literary readers. They are epical poems, but belong to the class of the self-conscious epic, and are far more Virgilian than Homeric. Homer gives us the heroes of that early age as they were. There is no attempt to avoid simplicity of detail; indeed in the *Odyssey* there is a distinct insistence on the minuter details of domestic life. But both Virgil and Tennyson made the background of their poems pictorial and romantic. As a matter of fact whatever events—if there is any rationalistic basis at all for the *Æneid* —took place in the story of Æneas, must have taken place with a sordid, savage background. But the scene is all laid among luxurious features, a settled and elaborate civilisation, in sunswept forest glades, or on mysterious headlands. The voluptuous detail of the Roman empire is freely lavished on the dwellings of barbarous kings and chieftains. Æneas himself bears about with him a treasure of in-

(195)

comparable richness, vessels of gold and silver, pictured tapestries, rich embroideries. Dido inhabits a patrician house of the Augustan period.

Tennyson applied the same treatment to his Arthurian legend; the scene is laid not in barbaric strongholds, rough fortresses, rude upland huts, but in dim cities, castles rich with carving. His knights ride in flashing armour or in sanguine stuffs, through enchanted forests and delicious glades, with here and there a cell or a monastery, with happy villages clustered at its base. The knights themselves are models of high courtesy and distinguished consideration, and speak in a way that betokens a liberal education.

The original scheme of the poems in Tennyson's mind seems to have been a mystical one, but in later life he was accustomed to manifest some impatience at any attempt to give precise allegorical interpretations to the poems.

He used to say impatiently, "I hate to be tied down to say, ' *This* means *that*,' because the thought within the image is much more than any one interpretation."

When the mystical interpretation of the *Idylls* was pressed, he said, "They have taken my hobby and ridden it too hard, and have explained some things too allegorically, although there is an allegorical, or perhaps rather parabolic drift in the poems."

He explained that the whole scheme of the *Idylls* was "the dream of man coming into practical life, and ruined by one sin. Birth is a mystery and death is a mystery, and in the midst lies the table-land of life, and its struggles and performances. It is not the history of one man or of one generation, but of a whole cycle of generations."

Speaking generally, then, it may be said that the *motif* of the whole is to display the thought of a noble idea formed, and to a certain extent carried out, but thwarted again and again by selfishness and sin, and closing in apparent failure, but yet sowing the seed of truth and purity through the land. Arthur's object is to establish law and order, civilisation in the highest sense, a high standard of unselfish and noble life. The attempt fails : his knights were meant to set a noble example of manliness, devotion and purity ; but the court teems with scandal, and finally the evil and seditious elements are triumphant.

The dominant note of the *Idylls* is of failure to realise great aims, and it will be noticed how many of the *Idylls* turn on base and painful tragedies. *Pelleas and Ettarre* depicts the sacrificing of a generous ideal to a selfish and sensual woman. In *Merlin and Vivien* age and wisdom fall a victim to a heartless wanton. *Balin and Balan* is an unrelieved tragedy. In *The Last Tournament* is the tale of the lawless love of Tristram and its punishment. In *Lancelot and Elaine,* which is another version of *The Lady of Shalott,* is the hopeless waste of a maiden love. In *Guinevere* is the doom of the faithless wife and the faithless friend. On the other hand the two idylls of *Geraint and Enid* give a beautiful and disconnected episode that bears little on the central story. *Gareth and Lynette* is a pretty romantic tale of chivalry. *The Holy Grail,* without doubt the most poetical, is the most mystical expression of the root-idea of the *Idylls.* *The Coming of Arthur* is prefatory, and the *Passing,* written first, where the noblest epical writing is to be found, gives the close of the great dream, with a hint of future triumph.

Thus it will be seen that there is no connected scheme in the poem. It is not an epic, it is a collection of episodes.

To make a general criticism of the *Idylls* it may be said at once that the narrative element is throughout better than the dramatic. The style is exquisitely clear, the lines are melodious, the ornament is profuse, yet not overloaded, the similes are not patches of splendour, but genuinely enlightening and illustrative touches.

The speeches it may be said are Virgilian—that is to say they are rhetorical; and here again we note them to be in many cases so elaborate as to be extremely obscure: occasionally, as in *Guinevere,* they are both moving and dignified;

but often they are apt to hinder the action, and alienate the attention rather than to concentrate and inspire it. I have often made the experiment of reading the *Idylls* aloud to boys of average intelligence, and while I find that the narrative passages enchain their attention, I have often found it necessary to omit whole sections of the speeches, simply because the meaning is so far from obvious at first hearing, and because they require so much comment and elucidation. Let a reader for instance turn to such a speech as Geraint makes to Enid's mother when he begs that Enid may wear her old dress :—

"O my new mother, be not wroth or grieved."

Beautiful as it is, and full of tender and pathetic lines, he will see that the rhetoric clouds the limpidity of the thought. Take such a passage as the following :—

> and I thought
> That could I someway prove such force in her
> Link'd with such love for me, that at a word
> (No reason given her) she could cast aside
> A splendour dear to women, new to her,
> And therefore dearer ; or if not so new,
> Yet therefore tenfold dearer by the power
> Of intermitted usage ; then I felt
> That I could rest, a rock in ebbs and flows,
> Fixt on her faith.

It is clear enough after a little thought what the passage means ; but it has not the simplicity of the true epic.　Doubtless Tennyson shrank before the baldness of realistic speech.

Again, when Limours renews his suit to Enid, the speech abounds in such lines as :—

> Owe you me nothing for a life half-lost ?
> Yea, yea, the whole dear debt of all you are.

> My malice is no deeper than a moat,
> No stronger than a wall : there is the keep ;
> He shall not cross us more.

Again Arthur's speech to his knights in *The Holy Grail*, when he returns and finds them aghast with the vision, is full of superficial obscurity, as in the lines :—

> But ye, that follow but the leader's bell,
> Taliessin is our fullest throat of song,
> And one hath sung and all the dumb will sing.

But no praise can be too high for the rich and sober grandeur of the narrative, the haunting magic that transplants the mind in an instant into the ancient world of dreams.　The exquisite comparisons, such as that where Geraint turns on the rabble rout of knights :—

> But at the flash and motion of the man
> They vanish'd panic-stricken, like a shoal
> Of darting fish, that on a summer morn
> Adown the crystal dykes at Camelot
> Come slipping o'er their shadows on the sand,
> But if a man who stands upon the brink
> But lift a shining hand against the sun,
> There is not left the twinkle of a fin
> Betwixt the cressy islets white in flower.

Or such a touch as

> And while he twangled, little Dagonet stood
> Quiet as any water-sodden log
> Stay'd in the wandering warble of a brook.

Or the novice in *Guinevere* describing how her father saw the fairies :—

> Himself beheld three spirits mad with joy
> Come dashing down on a tall wayside flower,
> That shook beneath them, as the thistle shakes
> When three gray linnets wrangle for the seed.

Or such descriptive passages as are thickly sown throughout the *Idylls*, like the following from *The Passing of Arthur* :—

> But the other swiftly strode from ridge to ridge,
> Clothed with his breath, and looking, as he walk'd,
> Larger than human on the frozen hills.
> He heard the deep behind him, and a cry
> Before. His own thought drove him like a goad.
> Dry clash'd his harness in the icy caves
> And barren chasms, and all to left and right
> The bare black cliff clang'd round him as he based
> His feet on juts of slippery crag that rang
> Sharp-smitten with the dint of armed heels—
> And on a sudden, lo ! the level lake,
> And the long glories of the winter moon.

This is the kind of writing that is pure magic, that sends a holy spectral shiver through the blood. And we may well read the *Idylls* over and over for such delights, as we may contentedly traverse weary leagues for the sight of some ancient tower or crystal fountain-head. All poetry cannot thrill

o

and move us equally, and even those who find
Arthur a solemn pedant, Lancelot a morbid slave
of passion, and Galahad an icy phantom, may
still put themselves within the reach of these wells
of healing. For such passages cannot be studied in
anthologies and selections; they must be found
flashing and gleaming in the bed-rock in which
they lie.

CHAPTER XIV

"POETRY," Tennyson once wrote, "should be the flower *and fruit* of a man's life, in whatever stage of it, to be a worthy offering to the world." These simple words contain the key to Tennyson's theory of the poetical life and character. Many accomplished poets have allowed poetry to be the flower and ornament of life, but have kept their serious hours, the *solidus dies*, for something more tangible and definite. Some singers, of whom Shelley is the prince, have sung wildly, impulsively, like an Æolian harp out of which the winds draw music, because their heart told them to sing, as the full-fed thrush sings on the high bare bough at evening. Tennyson had this impulse to sing; thought came to him in musical words; but he had a great deal more than this; he was, like Wordsworth, a deliberate, busy, strenuous poet; he gave up his life to poetry as another man may give it up to politics or commerce.

There were moods of depression, no doubt, such as come to all devoted men, when he asked himself what was the end of it all; what, when all was said and done, did he leave behind him? what did it all amount to? He must have been aware that the large mass of humanity regards poetry as a graceful accomplishment, as an amusement for a vacant hour, classing it with music, with the stage, with fiction, as the agreeable accompaniments of leisure,—"after the banquet the minstrel."

It was in such moods as these that he felt, as is recorded, an envy of hard practical workers, who left a tangible result. It was with such a thought as this in his mind that he told Dean Bradley, then Headmaster of Marlborough, that he envied him his life of hard, regular, useful, important work.

But there were other and higher moods in which no such misgivings troubled him, and when he felt that after all each man's work must be done in a corner; that a man must find out what part of the great sum of human work he can do best, and set to work quietly and soberly and diligently to do it; it was in this determination that Tennyson set about his poetry. Like the man in the Gospel story, the tree had to be dug about and nourished in a hard-handed, practical way; poetry was to be the fruit; the mellow, cool, nourishing produce of life and thought.

He looked earnestly forward, as he wrote in an early unpublished sonnet, to

A long day's dawn, when Poesy shall bind
Falsehood beneath the altar of great Truth.

The poet was after all the seer of truth; he was to enjoy leisure, to seclude himself from the world, to keep his eye clear to see the works of God, and to discern God behind them working silently, and walking in the garden in the cool of the day. The poet was to be the inspirer of earnest effort, he was to add to the humble toil of daily life the thrill, the glory that touches and consecrates all honest labour doggedly done, that beats the laborious ploughshare into the sword of the Spirit.

Through the silent early years a great ideal shaped itself in Tennyson's mind. He consecrated himself to the poetical life with strenuous aspiration, in no facile or indolent spirit, with no low appetite for personal success, but with a holy and severe dedication of all his powers to the one great end.

There are two poems, written with all the exuberant passion of youthful genius, which indicate the boundless possibilities that lie within the scope of poetry. *The Poet* is a manifesto, so to speak, of active poetical faith, and indicates in noble hyperbole the claims that the poet can make upon the outer world. The second—*The Poet's Mind*—shows how these results are to be achieved, the deep consecration, the passionate purity of life which the poet needs. Moreover in one of the latest volumes is included the poem—*Merlin and The Gleam*—which gives the retrospect, and shows the

old seer looking back upon life from the threshold
of the darkness, and describing the guiding light
which he has followed throughout.

It must be noted that in *The Poet* there is not
a trace of the theory of what has been recently
called the "self-effectuation" of art. It is held,
and strongly held by many, that art is an end in
itself; that to express beauty, or beautifully to
express what is not in itself beautiful, so long as it
be truly felt, is sufficient; that art, to use a
parable, should be content to flower, it may be in
the sight of men, it may be in lonely and unre-
garded places; but that the flowering is enough.
This theory is consistent with a very high ideal of
art—indeed it is claimed that the purity of
motive implied in whole-hearted devotion to art
without collateral aim is the highest ideal possible
to the artist. But it was not Tennyson's view. In
his mind the only ideal of art was the direct
service of humanity—art with him is strictly
subordinated to its effect on character, and the
artist is only justified if by the expression and interpretation of beauty he raises or attempts to raise
mankind into a higher range of feelings, a noble
ardour for things lovely and excellent, a deeper
devotion to truth, and a more reverent contemplation of the mysteries of God. He said once that
he had formed as he grew older the sorrowful
conviction that the English were beginning to

forget what was in Voltaire's words the glory of English poetry—"*No nation has treated in poetry moral ideas with more energy and depth than the English nation.*" The poet, in Tennyson's view, is the seer of pure visions :—

> He saw through life and death, thro' good and ill.

He shoots abroad, like some feathery-seeded plant, the arrows of his melodious thought,

> The winged shafts of *truth*,

and the flowers of his dreams are Freedom and Wisdom.

The second poem, *The Poet's Mind*, gives a picture of the soul from which these seeds are sown. It must be clear and bright ; it must be like a secluded garden, where a bright bird sings, and where a fountain leaps

> With a low melodious thunder.

The fountain must be fed with holiest truth of Heaven :—

> It is ever drawn
> From the brain of the purple mountain
> That stands in the distance yonder.
>
> .   .   .   .
>
> And the mountain draws it from Heaven above.

No "dark-browed sophist" must come near the sacred grove ; not only would he not guess at the secret of the place, but he would blight the flowers, and check the springing of the silvery stream.

In *The Gleam*, Merlin, the old prophet, near his end, looks back upon his earthly life. He tells how he was called to his work by an older and wise Magician :—

> And sweet the Magic
> When over the valley,
> In early summers,
> Over the mountain,
> On human faces,
> And all around me,
> Moving to melody,
> Floated The Gleam.

Then follows a time of discouragement, but the faith of the seer grows stronger and purer; through the wilderness and the stony mountain-tracks he comes out upon the plain and the hamlet, following the light that guides him. Then he comes to Camelot, and there "*rested* the Gleam."

By this Tennyson seems to signify that the *Idylls* contained the ideal essence of his teaching : for after this the Gleam passes on to the valley of the shadow, and the words are spoken in sight of the sea upon which he is so soon to embark.

We will now try to trace through hints given us in the *Memoir*, through scattered dicta, how this ideal was arrived at and how it was pursued. To a certain extent it may be said that a man's life is apt to follow the line of least resistance, and that it is apt to be the resultant of certain forces. Tennyson's temperament was hardly fitted for definite practical

work.   His love of nature and seclusion, his shyness,
the uncertain health of the earlier years all tended
to unfit him for any active practical occupation.
Indeed it is hard to suggest what line of life he
could have followed with success.   After his father's
death, too, it seemed as though it were a duty to
remain, for a time at all events, at home, and to
take as far as possible his father's place in the
bereaved household.   Moreover it was not absolutely necessary for him to earn a living.   Although
the absence of any adequate income obliged him to
defer all thoughts of marriage for many years, it
was still possible for him to live a life which was
neither unsociable nor undignified.   No doubt this
kind of life tended to develop in him a certain childlike vanity and self-absorption ; but it is impossible
to have the light without the shadow, and probably
there was hardly any life which could have given
such opportunities for self-development to a nature
such as his.   A certain amount of society was possible,
but it had to be sparingly indulged in and carefully
planned.   On the other hand his life gave him
opportunities for quiet profound meditation.   " I
require quiet, and myself to myself more than any
man when I write "—so he described his case in a
letter to his future wife.   Moreover he needed
much silent communing with Nature : he was ob-
servant, not, I believe, with the rapid restless
glance that seems, like a photographic plate, sensi-

tive to the smallest details of a scene; but he observed rather in a slow, tranquil and ruminative manner, and had a remarkable faculty for seizing upon the salient feature of a scene. He was, it must be remembered, exceedingly near-sighted, and what he observed was mostly detail on which, with a strong effort, he had concentrated and focussed his attention. Wordsworth used to say that it was his own way to study impartially all the details of a scene which struck his fancy; and that days after, when the vision had, so to speak, run clear, the characteristic details emerged in their true perfection in his mind; all else was forgotten and blurred. This was not Tennyson's way; he endeavoured, with the artist's instinct, to record at once in the most trenchant words his impressions of a scene; many of these lines and phrases were lost, floating away, as he once said, up the chimney on the fumes of his pipe. But some were preserved. In this way he not only stored his mind with poetical images, but these images had a precision which few poets attained.

But this was not all. It is clear that Tennyson possessed from the first the most exuberant faculty of imagination, and that not only was this faculty extraordinarily rich, but it was astonishingly precise. He said once that he could have drawn, had he the artistic gift, every scene in his poem with the minutest detail; and this faculty must have received some shocks from the illustrations of his poems and notably from the work of D. G. Rossetti, whose conceptions of the poems which he illustrated have the most determined tendency to embellish and even contradict the language of the poet. But Rossetti would have been the last person in the world to admit of any interference in his design. It is impossible, again, in the illustration which another eminent pre-Raphaelite made for *The Lady of Shalott*, not to wonder how Tennyson bore the interpretation of the "web" at which the lady was for ever weaving. In the poem it is obviously a tapestry, in which she weaves the sights, which reach her through the magic mirror. But in the illustration she is engaged in spinning on the floor a gigantic octagonal object like a spider's web, held down by large metal pins. For the purpose of embroidery, the lady could not by any mechanical device have reached the centre of this astonishing construction.

An interesting instance of the physical dominance of this imaginative faculty in Tennyson's case is given by himself in the experiences which resulted from a course of vegetarianism. He tried it, he said, for a short period, but broke down and turned with deep satisfaction to a mutton-chop—"I never felt such joy in my blood," he said. "When I went to sleep I dreamt that I saw the vines of the South with large Eshcol branches, trailing over the glaciers of the North."

This imaginative faculty was recognised from the first. Arthur Hallam in the early days wrote to him: "[Imagination is] with you universal and all-powerful, absorbing your whole existence, communicating to you that energy which is so glorious." But this faculty of pure imagination was not so strong as his power of entering into the sweet life of nature, and realising the sudden transient emotion that does not reside in the scene itself but in the heart of the observer. In the sensitive spirit there are chords so to speak that are sometimes tense, sometimes loose and languid; in the eager mood, the sight of some natural object, a tree, a hillside, a venerable house, a rock, a wave, will set these strings suddenly vibrating with a secret and inexplicable music. This is the mystery of the poetical nature; but of the thousands who feel such a thrill—and there are thousands—not more than one or two can give the mystic passion words. No language can give expression to the nature of this mysterious power; it fills the soul with music, it sets it afloat on a spiritual sea, which though remote from life seems in such moments to lie, with its sapphire firths and blue distances, among the arid craggy islands of daily existence. It is the voice of some higher power, the calling of the soul of the world; in such moments all is made clear, all harmonised and forgiven; the fact is incommunicable, but no one who has ever felt it can doubt of its reality, can question that it belongs to

some deeper mood, some higher plane of the spirit.
Many who in childhood and youth have felt the
beckoning of this mood, lose it in later life in contact with grosser realities; it cannot be counted
upon, it cannot be compelled; it may desert the
soul for years; and yet a voice, a sunset, a printed
page, a bar of music may bring it back.

These "authentic thrills" were what Tennyson set
himself resolutely to invite and cultivate.   He
speaks of his "dim mystic sympathies with tree and
hill reaching far back into childhood."   There was
a kind of religious sentiment in his mind about such
moments; Mr. Palgrave tells us that it was understood that when he was travelling with Tennyson,
if any scene of more than usual beauty met their
eyes, he was to withdraw for a few minutes and
allow the Poet to contemplate it in silence and solitude.   This was no pose, but a simple and natural
necessity of temperament; "I hear," said Tennyson once, "that there are larger waves at Bude than
at any other place.   I must go thither and be alone
with God."

After all, the question of whether or no a poet
fulfils the promise of his youth is not one which
admits of a decisive answer.   It all depends upon
the view taken by the particular critic, the particular reader, of the function and aim of the poet.
If you think of the poet as a teacher of morals, then
the more he drifts out of the irresponsible witchery

of song and steers into the stirring enunciation of rhetorical principles the more you will admire him. If your bent is towards realism, you will delight to find him a subtle analyst of character, a deft dissector of the human spirit, making its very deformities fascinating through the magic power of art. If you think of him as the teller of tales, you will deem him greater when he touches into life or eternal pathos some chivalrous or homely range of incident. But if you think of him as a priest of beauty, as a weaver of exquisite word-music stirring the sleeping soul into ripples of delicious sensation, then you will grudge your poet to the insistent cries of the world. You will desire for him enough of sympathy to encourage him to keep his lyre strung, and not so much of fame as to make him yield to the claims of those who would enlist his music in some urgent cause, which, however noble it may be in itself, is not the cause of that holy beauty of which the poet is the priest and minister.

My own belief is that FitzGerald was mainly right, and that Tennyson's real gift was the lyric gift. I believe that while he continued careless of name and fame he served his own ideal best; I believe that in his early lyrical poems, in *In Memoriam* and in *Maud*, his best work will be found; that in *The Princess*, the *Idylls*, the dramas, and the later poems, he was drawn aside from his real path by the pressure of public expectation, by social influences, by the noble desire to modify and direct thought. I do not underestimate the services he was enabled in these popular writings to do for his generation, but it can hardly be maintained that he was then practising his best gift. Not that Tennyson was consciously corrupted by fame or influence. It is clear that he always made the quality of his work his end, rather than any possible reward. But I suspect that he was overshadowed by a fictitious conscience; he was human, though a very large and simple character; and the atmosphere in which he lived was unreal and enervating. If he had not been a man of overpowering genius and childlike simplicity the effect upon him would have been disastrous. He would have become pontifical, self-conscious, elaborate. As it was his position only acted upon him with an uneasy pressure to write and think in ways that were not entirely consonant with the best of his genius.

I would think of Tennyson, then, not as the man of rank and name and fame, the associate of eminent persons, the embarrassed fugitive from peering curiosity, but as the lonely dreamer, lingering in still and secret places, listening to the music of woods, the plunge of stream and waves, the sighing of winds, with the airy music beating in his brain. This first; and then as heavily conscious of the deep and mysterious destiny of man, the bewildering mazes of identity, the bitter admixture of sorrow and pain with the very draught of life. He stands on the edge of the abyss; he looks with faltering eyes into the dark, and the thin voice of death, the sobbing of despair, the cries of unsoothed pain tell him that the dark is not lifeless, that there is something beyond and above and around all, and that the same eternal, awful Power which laughs in the sunlight, which touches the flower with the distilled flush of the heavenly ray, is as present in darkness as in light, and bears upon his un- wearied shoulder the infinite multitude of stars and suns, and enfolds all things within himself.

On the one hand beauty, the beauty that triumphs over the petty, busy handiwork of man, and on the other mystery, the mystery from which man comes and into which he goes.

⁎ I am enabled to print the two poems that follow, *The Palace of Art* and *The Lady of Shalott,* with all variations in the text, by the kind permission of Mr. Churton Collins.

APPENDIX

[*The Palace of Art* and *The Lady of Shalott* with the various readings; from *The Early Poems of Alfred Lord Tennyson*, text of 1857, edited by John Churton Collins.]

THE PALACE OF ART

I BUILT my soul a lordly pleasure-house,
    Wherein at ease for aye to dwell.
I said, "O Soul, make merry and carouse,
    Dear soul, for all is well."

A huge crag-platform, smooth as burnish'd brass,
    I chose. The ranged ramparts bright
From level meadow-bases of deep grass [1]
    Suddenly scaled the light.

Thereon I built it firm. Of ledge or shelf
    The rock rose clear, or winding stair.
My soul would live alone unto herself
    In her high palace there.

And "while the world [2] runs round and round," I said,
    "Reign thou apart, a quiet king,
Still as, while Saturn whirls, his stedfast [3] shade
    Sleeps on his luminous ring." [4]

To which my soul made answer readily:
    "Trust me, in bliss I shall abide
In this great mansion, that is built for me,
    So royal-rich and wide."

[1] 1833. I chose, whose rangèd ramparts bright
    From great broad meadow bases of deep grass.
[2] 1833. "While the great world."
[3] 1833 and 1842. Steadfast.
[4] After this stanza in 1833 this, deleted in 1842:—
    "And richly feast within thy palace hall,
      Like to the dainty bird that sups,
    Lodged in the lustrous crown-imperial,
      Draining the honey cups."

P

* * * * * * * * *
* * * * * * * * *

Four courts I made, East, West and South and North,
  In each a squared lawn, wherefrom
The golden gorge of dragons spouted forth
  A flood of fountain-foam.[1]

And round the cool green courts there ran a row
  Of cloisters, branch'd like mighty woods,
Echoing all night to that sonorous flow
  Of spouted fountain-floods.[1]

And round the roofs a gilded gallery
  That lent broad verge to distant lands,
Far as the wild swan wings, to where the sky
  Dipt down to sea and sands.[1]

From those four jets four currents in one swell
  Across the mountain stream'd below
In misty folds, that floating as they fell
  Lit up a torrent-bow.[1]

And high on every peak a statue seem'd
  To hang on tiptoe, tossing up
A cloud of incense of all odour steam'd
  From out a golden cup.[1]

So that she thought, "And who shall gaze upon
  My palace with unblinded eyes,
While this great bow will waver in the sun,
  And that sweet incense rise?"[1]

For that sweet incense rose and never fail'd,
  And, while day sank or mounted higher,
The light aërial gallery, golden-rail'd,
  Burnt like a fringe of fire.[1]

Likewise the deep-set windows, stain'd and traced,
  Would seem slow-flaming crimson fires
From shadow'd grots of arches interlaced,
  And tipt with frost-like spires.[1]

---

[1] In 1833 these eight stanzas were inserted after the stanza beginning, "I take possession of men's minds and deeds;" in 1842 they were transferred, greatly altered, to their present position. For the alterations on them see *infra*, pages 224, 225.

*   *   *   *   *   *   *   *   *
*   *   *   *   *   *   *   *   *

Full of long-sounding corridors it was,
    That over-vaulted grateful gloom,[1]
Thro' which the livelong day my soul did pass,
    Well-pleased, from room to room.

Full of great rooms and small the palace stood,
    All various, each a perfect whole
From living Nature, fit for every mood[2]
    And change of my still soul.

For some were hung with arras green and blue,
    Showing a gaudy summer-morn,
Where with puff'd cheek the belted hunter blew
    His wreathed bugle-horn.[3]

One seem'd all dark and red—a tract of sand,
    And some one pacing there alone,
Who paced for ever in a glimmering land,
    Lit with a low large moon.[4]

One show'd an iron coast and angry waves.
    You seem'd to hear them climb and fall
And roar rock-thwarted under bellowing caves,
    Beneath the windy wall.[5]

[1] 1833. Gloom,
    Roofed with thick plates of green and orange glass
        Ending in stately rooms.

[2] 1833. All various, all beautiful,
        Looking all ways, fitted to every mood.

[3] Here in 1833 was inserted the stanza, "One showed an English home," afterwards transferred to its present position as stanza 22.

[4] 1833. Some were all dark and red, a glimmering land
        Lit with a low round moon,
    Among brown rocks a man upon the sand
        Went weeping all alone.

[5] This stanza was added in 1842.

And one, a full-fed river winding slow
  By herds upon an endless plain,
The ragged rims of thunder brooding low,
  With shadow-streaks of rain.[1]

And one, the reapers at their sultry toil.
  In front they bound the sheaves. Behind
Were realms of upland, prodigal in oil,
  And hoary to the wind.[1]

And one, a foreground black with stones and slags,
  Beyond, a line of heights, and higher
All barr'd with long white cloud the scornful crags,
  And highest, snow and fire.[2]

And one, an English home—gray twilight pour'd
  On dewy pastures, dewy trees,
Softer than sleep—all things in order stored,
  A haunt of ancient Peace.[3]

Nor these alone, but every landscape fair,
  As fit for every mood of mind,
Or gay, or grave, or sweet, or stern, was there,
  Not less than truth design'd.[4]

*　　*　　*　　*　　*　　*　　*　　*　　*
*　　*　　*　　*　　*　　*　　*　　*　　*

Or the maid-mother by a crucifix,
  In tracts of pasture sunny-warm,

[1] These two stanzas were added in 1842.
[2] Thus in 1833 :—
    One seemed a foreground black with stones and slags,
      Below sun-smitten icy spires
    Rose striped with long white cloud the scornful crags,
      Deep trenched with thunder fires.
[3] Not inserted here in 1833, but the following in its place :—
    Some showed far-off thick woods mounted with towers,
      Nearer, a flood of mild sunshine
    Poured on long walks and lawns and beds and bowers
      Trellised with bunchy vine.
[4] Inserted in 1842.

Beneath branch-work of costly sardonyx
 Sat smiling, babe in arm.[1]

Or in a clear-wall'd city on the sea,
 Near gilded organ-pipes, her hair
Wound with white roses, slept St. Cecily ;
 An angel look'd at her.

[1] Thus in 1833, followed by the note :—
> Or the maid-mother by a crucifix,
> In yellow pastures sunny-warm,
> Beneath branch-work of costly sardonyx,
> Sat smiling, babe in arm.[*]

[*] When I first conceived the plan of the Palace of Art, I intended to have introduced both sculptures and paintings into it :
but it is the most difficult of all things to *devise* a statue in verse.
Judge whether I have succeeded in the statues of Elijah and
Olympias.

> One was the Tishbite whom the raven fed,
> As when he stood on Carmel steeps,
> With one arm stretched out bare, and mocked and said,
> "Come cry aloud—he sleeps."
>
> Tall, eager, lean and strong, his cloak wind-borne
> Behind, his forehead heavenly bright
> From the clear marble pouring glorious scorn,
> Lit as with inner light.
>
> One was Olympias : the floating snake
> Rolled round her ancles, round her waist
> Knotted, and folded once about her neck,
> Her perfect lips to taste.
>
> Round by the shoulder moved : she seeming blythe
> Declined her head : on every side
> The dragon's curves melted and mingled with
> The woman's youthful pride
> Of rounded limbs.
>
> Or Venus in a snowy shell alone,
> Deep-shadowed in the glassy brine,
> Moonlike glowed double on the blue, and shone
> A naked shape divine.

Or thronging all one porch of Paradise,
  A group of Houris bow'd to see
The dying Islamite, with hands and eyes
  That said, We wait for thee.[1]

Or mythic Uther's deeply-wounded son
  In some fair space of sloping greens
Lay, dozing in the vale of Avalon,
  And watch'd by weeping queens.[2]

Or hollowing one hand against his ear,
  To list a foot-fall, ere he saw
The wood-nymph, stay'd the Ausonian king to hear
  Of wisdom and of law.[3]

Or over hills with peaky tops engrail'd,
  And many a tract of palm and rice,
The throne of Indian Cama[4] slowly sail'd
  A summer fann'd with spice.

[1] Inserted in 1842.

[2] Thus in 1833 :—

    Or that deep-wounded child of Pendragon
      Mid misty woods on sloping greens
    Dozed in the valley of Avilion,
      Tended by crownèd queens.

The present reading that of 1842. The reference is, of course
to King Arthur, the supposed son of Uther Pendragon.
In 1833 the following stanza, excised in 1842, followed :—

    Or blue-eyed Kriemhilt from a craggy hold,
      Athwart the light-green rows of vine,
    Poured blazing hoards of Nibelungen gold,
      Down to the gulfy Rhine.

[3] Inserted in 1842 thus :—

    Or hollowing one hand against his ear,
      To listen for a footfall, ere he saw
    The wood-nymph, stay'd the Tuscan king to hear
      Of wisdom and of law.

List a footfall, 1843. Ausonian for Tuscan, 1850.

[4] Camadev, the Hindu God of Love.

Or sweet Europa's mantle blew unclasp'd,
From off her shoulder backward borne :
From one hand droop'd a crocus : one hand grasp'd
The mild bull's golden horn.[1]

Or else flush'd Ganymede, his rosy thigh
Half-buried in the Eagle's down,
Sole as a flying star shot thro' the sky
Above[2] the pillar'd town.

Nor[3] these alone : but every[4] legend fair
Which the supreme Caucasian mind
Carved out of Nature for itself, was there,
Not less than life, design'd.[5]

---

[1] In 1833 thus :—
    Europa's scarf blew in an arch, unclasped,
        From her bare shoulder backward borne.
"Off" inserted in 1842.
Here in 1833 follows a stanza, excised in 1842 :—
    He thro' the streaming crystal swam, and rolled
        Ambrosial breaths that seemed to float
    In light-wreathed curls. She from the ripple cold
        Updrew her sandalled foot.
[2] 1833. Over.   [3] 1833. Not.   [4] 1833. Many a.
[5] 1833. Broidered in screen and blind.
In the edition of 1833 appear the following stanzas, excised
in 1842 :—
    So that my soul beholding in her pride
        All these, from room to room did pass ;
    And all things that she saw, she multiplied,
        A many-facèd glass.

    And, being both the sower and the seed,
        Remaining in herself became
    All that she saw, Madonna, Ganymede,
        Or the Asiatic dame—

    Still changing, as a lighthouse in the night
        Changeth athwart the gleaming main,
    From red to yellow, yellow to pale white,
        Then back to red again.

*   *   *   *   *   *   *   *   *
*   *   *   *   *   *   *   *   *

Then in the towers I placed great bells that swung,
  Moved of themselves, with silver sound ;
And with choice paintings of wise men I hung
  The royal daïs round.

"From change to change four times within the womb
  The brain is moulded," she began,
"So thro' all phases of all thought I come
  Into the perfect man.*

"All nature widens upward : evermore
  The simpler essence lower lies,
More complex is more perfect, owning more
  Discourse, more widely wise.*

"I take possession of men's minds and deeds.
  I live in all things great and small.
I dwell apart, holding no forms of creeds,
  But contemplating all." †

Four ample courts there were, East, West, South, North,
  In each a squarèd lawn where from
A golden-gorgèd dragon spouted forth
  The fountain's diamond foam.

All round the cool green courts there ran a row
  Of cloisters, branched like mighty woods,
Echoing all night to that sonorous flow
  Of spouted fountain floods.

From those four jets four currents in one swell
  Over the black rock streamed below
In steamy folds, that, floating as they fell,
  Lit up a torrent-bow.

And round the roofs ran gilded galleries
  That gave large view to distant lands,
Tall towns and mounds, and close beneath the skies
  Long lines of amber sands.

Huge incense-urns along the balustrade,
  Hollowed of solid amethyst,
Each with a different odour fuming, made
  The air a silver mist.

*These two excised stanzas, with minute alterations, were
incorporated with the poem a few stanzas further down in 1842.
See pages 228, 229.
  †See page 229.

For there was Milton like a seraph strong,
  Beside him Shakespeare bland and mild ;
And there the world-worn Dante grasp'd his song,
  And somewhat grimly smiled.[1]

  Far-off 'twas wonderful to look upon
    Those sumptuous towers between the gleam
  Of that great foam-bow trembling in the sun,
    And the argent incense-stream ;

  And round the terraces and round the walls,
    While day sank lower or rose higher,
  To see those rails, with all their knobs and balls,
    Burn like a fringe of fire.

  Likewise the deepset windows, stained and traced,
    Burned, like slow-flaming crimson fires,
  From shadowed grots of arches interlaced,
    And topped with frostlike spires.

[1] 1833.   There deep-haired Milton like an angel tall
        Stood limnèd, Shakspeare bland and mild,
      Grim Dante pressed his lips, and from the wall
        The bald blind Homer smiled.

  Recast in its present form in 1842.   After this stanza in 1833
appear the following stanzas, excised in 1842 :—
        And underneath fresh carved in cedar wood,
          Somewhat alike in form and face,
        The Genii of every climate stood,
          All brothers of one race :

        Angels who sway the seasons by their art,
          And mould all shapes in earth and sea ;
        And with great effort build the human heart
          From earliest infancy.

        And in the sun-pierced Oriels' coloured flame
          Immortal Michæl Angelo
        Looked down, bold Luther, large-browed Verulam,
          The King of those who know.

        Cervantes, the bright face of Calderon,
          Robed David touching holy strings,
        The Halicarnassean, and alone,
          Alfred the flower of kings.

        Isaiah with fierce Ezekiel,
          Swarth Moses by the Coptic sea,
        Plato, Petrarca, Livy, and Raphael,
          And eastern Confutzee.

And there the Ionian father of the rest;
   A million wrinkles carved his skin;
A hundred winters snow'd upon his breast,
   From cheek and throat and chin.[1]

Above, the fair hall-ceiling stately set
   Many an arch high up did lift,
And angels rising and descending met
   With interchange of gift.[1]

Below was all mosaic choicely plann'd
   With cycles of the human tale
Of this wide world, the times of every land
   So wrought, they will not fail.[1]

The people here, a beast of burden slow,
   Toil'd onward, prick'd with goads and stings;
Here play'd, a tiger, rolling to and fro
   The heads and crowns of kings;[1]

Here rose, an athlete, strong to break or bind
   All force in bonds that might endure,
And here once more like some sick man declined,
   And trusted any cure.[1]

But over these she trod: and those great bells
   Began to chime. She took her throne:
She sat betwixt the shining Oriels,
   To sing her songs alone.[1]

And thro' the topmost Oriels' colour'd flame
   Two godlike faces gazed below;
Plato the wise, and large-brow'd Verulam,
   The first of those who know.[1]

----

[1] All these stanzas were added in 1842. In 1833 appear the following stanzas, excised in 1842:—
   As some rich tropic mountain that infolds
      All change, from flats of scattered palms
   Sloping thro' five great zones of climate, holds
      His head in snows and calms—

   Full of her own delight and nothing else,
      My vainglorious, gorgeous soul
   Sat throned between the shining oriels,
      In pomp beyond control;

And all those names, that in their motion were
Full-welling fountain-heads of change,

    With piles of flavorous fruits in basket-twine
      Of gold, unheapèd, crushing down
    Musk-scented blooms—all taste—grape, gourd or pine—
      In bunch, or single grown—

    Our growths, and such as brooding Indian heats
      Make out of crimson blossoms deep,
    Ambrosial pulps and juices, sweets from sweets
      Sun-changed, when sea-winds sleep.

    With graceful chalices of curious wine,
      Wonders of art—and costly jars,
    And bossèd salvers. Ere young night divine
      Crowned dying day with stars,

    Making sweet close of his delicious toils,
      She lit white streams of dazzling gas,
    And soft and fragrant flames of precious oils
      In moons of purple glass

    Ranged on the fretted woodwork to the ground.
      Thus her intense untold delight,
    In deep or vivid colour, smell and sound,
      Was flattered day and night.*

   * If the poem were not already too long, I should have inserted in the text the following stanzas, expressive of the joy wherewith the soul contemplated the results of astronomical experiment. In the centre of the four quadrangles rose an immense tower.

    Hither, when all the deep unsounded skies
      Shuddered with silent stars she clomb,
    And as with optic glasses her keen eyes
      Pierced thro' the mystic dome,

    Regions of lucid matter taking forms,
      Brushes of fire, hazy gleams,
    Clusters and beds of worlds, and bee-like swarms
      Of suns, and starry streams.

    She saw the snowy poles of moonless Mars,
      That marvellous round of milky light
    Below Orion, and those double stars
      Whereof the one more bright

    Is circled by the other, etc.

Betwixt the slender shafts were blazon'd fair
    In diverse raiment strange: [1]

Thro' which the lights, rose, amber, emerald, blue,
    Flush'd in her temples and her eyes,
And from her lips, as morn from Memnon, drew
    Rivers of melodies.

No nightingale delighteth to prolong
    Her low preamble all alone,
More than my soul to hear her echo'd song
    Throb thro' the ribbed stone;

Singing and murmuring in her feastful mirth,
    Joying to feel herself alive,
Lord over Nature, Lord of [2] the visible earth,
    Lord of the senses five;

Communing with herself; "All these are mine,
    And let the world have peace or wars,
'Tis one to me." She—when young night divine
    Crown'd dying day with stars,

Making sweet close of his delicious toils—
    Lit light in wreaths and anadems,
And pure quintessences of precious oils
    In hollow'd moons of gems,

To mimic heaven; and clapt her hands and cried,
    "I marvel if my still delight
In this great house so royal-rich, and wide,
    Be flatter'd to the height.[3]

[1] Thus in 1833:—
        And many more, that in their lifetime were
            Full-welling fountain heads of change,
        Between the stone shafts glimmered, blazoned fair
            In divers raiment strange.
[2] 1833. O'.
[3] Here added in 1842 and remaining till 1851 when they were
excised are two stanzas :—
        "From shape to shape at first within the womb
            The brain is modell'd," she began,
        "And thro' all phases of all thought I come
            Into the perfect man.

" O all things fair to sate my various eyes !
O shapes and hues that please me well !
O silent faces of the Great and Wise,
    My Gods, with whom I dwell ! [1]

" O God-like isolation which art mine,
    I can but count thee perfect gain,
What time I watch the darkening droves of swine
    That range on yonder plain. [1]

" In filthy sloughs they roll a prurient skin,
    They graze and wallow, breed and sleep ;
And oft some brainless devil enters in,
    And drives them to the deep." [1]

Then of the moral instinct would she prate,
    And of the rising from the dead,
As hers by right of full-accomplish'd Fate ;
    And at the last she said :

" I take possession of man's mind and deed.
    I care not what the sects may brawl,
I sit as God holding no form of creed,
    But contemplating all." [2]

* * * * * * * * *
* * * * * * * * *

" All nature widens upward. Evermore
The simpler essence lower lies :
More complex is more perfect, owning more
Discourse, more widely wise."

[1] These stanzas were added in 1851.
[2] Added here in 1842 [though originally written in 1833 and placed earlier in the poem. See page 224], with the following variants which remained till 1851, when the present text was substituted :—
    " I take possession of men's minds and deeds.
    I live in all things great and small.
I sit * apart holding no forms of creeds,
    But contemplating all."

* * * * * * * * *
* * * * * * * * *

* 1833. Dwell.

Full oft[1] the riddle of the painful earth
 Flash'd thro' her as she sat alone,
Yet not the less held she her solemn mirth,
 And intellectual throne.

And so she throve and prosper'd : so three years
 She prosper'd : on the fourth she fell[2]
Like Herod, when the shout was in his ears,
 Struck thro' with pangs of hell.

Lest she should fail and perish utterly,
 God, before whom ever lie bare
The abysmal deeps of Personality,
 Plagued her with sore despair.

When she would think, where'er she turn'd her sight,
 The airy hand confusion wrought,
Wrote "Mene, mene," and divided quite
 The kingdom of her thought.

Deep dread and loathing of her solitude
 Fell on her, from which mood was born
Scorn of herself; again, from out that mood
 Laughter at her self-scorn.[3]

"What! is not this my place of strength," she said,
 "My spacious mansion built for me,
Whereof the strong foundation-stones were laid
 Since my first memory?"

[1] 1833. Sometimes.

[2] And intellectual throne

    Of full-sphered contemplation. So three years
      She throve, but on the fourth she fell.

And so the text remained till 1850, when the present reading was substituted.

[3] In 1833 the following stanza, excised in 1842 :—

    "Who hath drawn dry the fountains of delight,
      That from my deep heart everywhere
    Moved in my blood and dwelt, as power and might
      Abode in Sampson's hair?"

But in dark corners of her palace stood
   Uncertain shapes ; and unawares
On white-eyed phantasms weeping tears of blood,
   And horrible nightmares,

And hollow shades enclosing hearts of flame,
   And, with dim fretted foreheads all,
On corpses three-months-old at noon she came,
   That stood against the wall.

A spot of dull stagnation, without light
   Or power of movement, seem'd my soul,
'Mid onward-sloping [1] motions infinite
   Making for one sure goal.

A still salt pool, lock'd in with bars of sand ;
   Left on the shore ; that hears all night
The plunging seas draw backward from the land
   Their moon-led waters white.

A star that with the choral starry dance
   Join'd not, but stood, and standing saw
The hollow orb of moving Circumstance
   Roll'd round by one fix'd law.

Back on herself her serpent pride had curl'd.
   "No voice," she shriek'd in that lone hall,
"No voice breaks thro' the stillness of this world :
   One deep, deep silence all ! "

She, mouldering with the dull earth's mouldering sod,
   Inwrapt tenfold in slothful shame,
Lay there exiled from eternal God,
   Lost to her place and name ;

And death and life she hated equally,
   And nothing saw, for her despair,
But dreadful time, dreadful eternity,
   No comfort anywhere ;

[1] 1833. Downward-sloping.

Remaining utterly confused with fears,
 And ever worse with growing time,
And ever unrelieved by dismal tears,
 And all alone in crime :

Shut up as in a crumbling tomb, girt round
 With blackness as a solid wall,
Far off she seem'd to hear the dully sound
 Of human footsteps fall.

As in strange lands a traveller walking slow,
 In doubt and great perplexity,
A little before moon-rise hears the low
 Moan of an unknown sea ;

And knows not if it be thunder or a sound
 Of rocks [1] thrown down, or one deep cry
Of great wild beasts ; then thinketh, " I have found
 A new land, but I die."

She howl'd aloud, "I am on fire within.
 There comes no murmur of reply.
What is it that will take away my sin,
 And save me lest I die?"

So when four years were wholly finished,
 She threw her royal robes away.
" Make me a cottage in the vale," she said,
 "Where I may mourn and pray. [2]

"Yet pull not down my palace towers, that are
 So lightly, beautifully built:
Perchance I may return with others there
 When I have purged my guilt."

[1] 1833.   Or the sound
         Of stones.
So till 1851, when "a sound of rocks" was substituted.
         [2] 1833. "Dying the death I die?"
Present reading substituted in 1842.

THE LADY OF SHALOTT

First published in 1833

PART I

ON either side the river lie
Long fields of barley and of rye,
That clothe the wold and meet the sky;
And thro' the field the road runs by
      To many-tower'd Camelot;
And up and down the people go,
Gazing where the lilies blow
Round an island there below,
      The island of Shalott.[1]

Willows whiten, aspens quiver,[2]
Little breezes dusk and shiver
Thro' the wave that runs for ever
By the island in the river
      Flowing down to Camelot.
Four gray walls, and four gray towers,
Overlook a space of flowers,
And the silent isle imbowers
      The Lady of Shalott.

By the margin, willow-veil'd
Slide the heavy barges trail'd
By slow horses; and unhail'd
The shallop flitteth silken-sail'd
      Skimming down to Camelot:

[1] 1833.   To many towered Camelot
      The yellow leavèd water lily,
      The green sheathed daffodilly,
      Tremble in the water chilly,
         Round about Shalott.
[2] 1833.   shiver,
      The sunbeam-showers break and quiver
      In the stream that runneth ever
      By the island, etc.

But who hath seen her wave her hand?
Or at the casement seen her stand?
Or is she known in all the land,
   The Lady of Shalott?[1]

Only reapers, reaping early
In among the bearded barley,
Hear a song that echoes cheerly
From the river winding clearly,
   Down to tower'd Camelot:
And by the moon the reaper weary,
Piling sheaves in uplands airy,
Listening, whispers " 'Tis the fairy
   Lady of Shalott ".[2]

Part II

THERE she weaves by night and day
A magic web with colours gay.
She has heard a whisper say,
A curse is on her if she stay[3]

[1] 1833. Underneath the bearded barley,
   The reaper, reaping late and early,
   Hears her ever chanting cheerly,
   Like an angel, singing clearly,
    O'er the stream of Camelot.
   Piling the sheaves in furrows airy,
   Beneath the moon, the reaper weary
   Listening whispers, "'tis the fairy
    Lady of Shalott."
[2] 1833. The little isle is all inrailed
   With a rose-fence, and overtrailed
   With roses: by the marge unhailed
   The shallop flitteth silkensailed,
    Skimming down to Camelot.
   A pearl garland winds her head:
   She leaneth on a velvet bed,
   Full royally apparellèd,
    The Lady of Shalott.
[3] 1833. No time hath she to sport and play:
   A charmèd web she weaves alway.
   A curse is on her, if she stay
   Her weaving, either night or day

To look down to Camelot.
She knows not what the curse may be,
And so[1] she weaveth steadily,
And little other care hath she,
   The Lady of Shalott.

And moving thro' a mirror clear
That hangs before her all the year,
Shadows of the world appear.
There she sees the highway near
   Winding down to Camelot:
There the river eddy whirls,
And there the surly village-churls,[2]
And the red cloaks of market girls,
   Pass onward from Shalott.

Sometimes a troop of damsels glad,
An abbot on an ambling pad,
Sometimes a curly shepherd-lad,
Or long-hair'd page in crimson clad,
   Goes by to tower'd Camelot;
And sometimes thro' the mirror blue
The knights come riding two and two:
She hath no loyal knight and true,
   The Lady of Shalott.

But in her web she still delights
To weave the mirror's magic sights,
For often thro' the silent nights
A funeral, with plumes and lights,
   And music, went to Camelot:[3]

[1] 1833. Therefore . . .
    Therefore no other. . .
     The Lady of Shalott.
[2] 1833. She lives with little joy or fear
    Over the water running near,
    The sheep bell tinkles in her ear,
    Before her hangs a mirror clear,
     Reflecting towered Camelot.
    And, as the mazy web she whirls,
    She sees the surly village-churls.
[3] 1833. Came from Camelot.

Or when the moon was overhead,
Came two young lovers lately wed
"I am half-sick of shadows," said
    The Lady of Shalott.

PART III

A BOW-SHOT from her bower-eaves,
He rode between the barley sheaves,
The sun came dazzling thro' the leaves,
And flamed upon the brazen greaves
    Of bold Sir Lancelot.
A redcross knight for ever kneel'd
To a lady in his shield,
That sparkled on the yellow field,
    Beside remote Shalott.

The gemmy bridle glitter'd free,
Like to some branch of stars we see
Hung in the golden Galaxy.[1]
The bridle bells rang merrily
    As he rode down to [2] Camelot:
And from his blazon'd baldric slung
A mighty silver bugle hung,
And as he rode his armour rung,
    Beside remote Shalott.

All n the blue unclouded weather
Thick-jewell'd shone the saddle-leather,
The helmet and the helmet-feather
Burn'd like one burning flame together,
    As he rode down to Camelot.[3]
As often thro' the purple night,
Below the starry clusters bright,
Some bearded meteor, trailing light,
    Moves over still Shalott.[4]

---

[1] 1833. Hung in the golden galaxy.   [2] 1833. From.
[3] 1833. From Camelot.   [4] 1833. Green Shalott.

His broad clear brow in sunlight glow'd ;
On burnish'd hooves his war-horse trode ;
From underneath his helmet flow'd
His coal-black curls as on he rode,
      As he rode down to Camelot.[1]
From the bank and from the river
He flashed into the crystal mirror,
"Tirra lirra," by the river [2]
      Sang Sir Lancelot.

She left the web, she left the loom ;
She made three paces thro' the room,
She saw the water-lily [3] bloom.
She saw the helmet and the plume,
      She look'd down to Camelot.
Out flew the web and floated wide ;
The mirror crack'd from side to side ;
"The curse is come upon me," cried
      The Lady of Shalott.

PART IV

In the stormy east-wind straining,
The pale yellow woods were waning,
The broad stream in his banks complaining,
Heavily the low sky raining
      Over tower'd Camelot ;
Down she came and found a boat
Beneath a willow left afloat,
And round about the prow she wrote
      The Lady of Shalott.[4]

And now the river's dim expanse—
Like some bold seër in a trance,

[1] 1833. From Camelot.   [2] 1833. "Tirra lirra, tirra lirra."
[3] 1833. Water flower.
    [4] 1833. Outside the isle a shallow boat
            Beneath a willow lay afloat
            Below the carven stern she wrote,
               THE LADY OF SHALOTT.

Seeing all his own mischance—
With a glassy countenance
   Did she look to Camelot.
And at the closing of the day
She loosed the chain, and down she lay ;
The broad stream bore her far away,
   The Lady of Shalott.

Lying, robed in snowy white
That loosely flew to left and right—
The leaves upon her falling light—
Thro' the noises of the night
   She floated down to Camelot ;
And as the boat-head wound along
The willowy hills and fields among,
They heard her singing her last song,
   The Lady of Shalott.[1]

[1] 1833. A cloud-white crown of pearl she dight,
  All raimented in snowy white
  That loosely flew (her zone in sight,
  Clasped with one blinding diamond bright),
   Her wide eyes fixed on Camelot,
  Though the squally eastwind keenly
  Blew, with folded arms serenely
  By the water stood the queenly
   Lady of Shalott.

  With a steady, stony glance—
  Like some bold seer in a trance,
  Beholding all his own mischance,
  Mute, with a glassy countenance—
   She looked down to Camelot.
  It was the closing of the day,
  She loosed the chain, and down she lay,
  The broad stream bore her far away,
   The Lady of Shalott.

  As when to sailors while they roam,
  By creeks and outfalls far from home,
  Rising and dropping with the foam,
  From dying swans wild warblings come,
   Blown shoreward ; so to Camelot

Heard a carol, mournful, holy,
Chanted loudly, chanted lowly,
Till her blood was frozen slowly,
And her eyes were darken'd wholly,[1]
    Turn'd to tower'd Camelot;
For ere she reach'd upon the tide
The first house by the water-side,
Singing in her song she died,
    The Lady of Shalott.

Under tower and balcony,
By garden-wall and gallery,
A gleaming shape she floated by,
Dead-pale[2] between the houses high,
    Silent into Camelot.
Out upon the wharfs they came,
Knight and burgher, lord and dame,
And round the prow they read her name,
    The Lady of Shalott.[3]

Who is this? and what is here?
And in the lighted palace near
Died the sound of royal cheer;
And they cross'd themselves for fear,
    All the knights at Camelot ·

    Still as the boat-head wound along
    The willowy hills and fields among,
    They heard her chanting her death song,
    The Lady of Shalott.

[1] 1833. A long drawn carol, mournful, holy,
    She chanted loudly, chanted lowly,
    Till her eyes were darkened wholly.
    And her smooth face sharpened slowly.

[2] "A corse" (1853) is a variant for the "Dead-pale" of 1857.

[3] 1833. A pale, pale corpse she floated by,
    Dead cold, between the houses high,
      Dead into towered Camelot.
    Knight and burgher, lord and dame,
    To the plankèd wharfage came:
    Below the stern they read her name,
      "The Lady of Shalott."

But Lancelot[1] mused a little space;
He said, "She has a lovely face;
God in his mercy lend her grace,
        The Lady of Shalott".[2]

[1] 1833.   Spells it "Launcelot" all through.
[2] 1833.   They crossed themselves, their stars they blest,
            Knight, minstrel, abbot, squire and guest,
            There lay a parchment on her breast,
            That puzzled more than all the rest,
                The well-fed wits at Camelot.
            " *The web was woven curiously,*
            The charm is broken utterly,
            Draw near and fear not—this is I,
                The Lady of Shalott."

INDEX

Aldworth, Tennyson's house near Haslemere, 48.
Alexandra, Queen, Tennyson's interview with, 102.
Alford, Dean, 8.
Allen, Dr., 26.
Allingham, William, 15, 65.
"Apostles," the, a society, 9.
Arnold, Matthew, 130.
Astronomy, Tennyson's love of, 5, 83.
Austen, Jane, 98.

Blakesley, Dean, 8.
Boxley, home of Tennyson family, 20.
Boyd, Mr., 11.
Bradley, Dean, 47, 66.
Brassey, Lord, 73.
Browning, Robert, 41, 60; death of, 74; Tennyson's criticism of writings, 130.
Browning, Mrs., 30.
Bryce, James, 60.
Burns, Robert, 129.
Byron, Lord, poetical influence over Tennyson, 127.

Cambridge, Tennyson's life at, 7-11; elected Hon. Fellow, 50; lines on Cambridge of 1830, quoted, 11.
Campbell, Thomas, 22.
Carlyle, 2, 22, 27, 31, 62.
Chancellor's medal won by Tennyson, 10.
Cheltenham, home of Tennyson family, 20, 30.
Clark, Sir Andrew, 63, 72.
Collins, Churton, 153.
Cornwall, Tennyson's visit to, 32.
Currie, Sir Donald, 66.
Csar and Czarina, 67.

Dante, 132.
De Musset, Alfred, 148.
Denmark, King and Queen of, Tennyson's meeting with, 67.
De Vere, Aubrey, 35, 138.
D'Eyncourt, 1.
Dickens, 22, 25.
Disraeli [Lord Beaconsfield], 54.
Dobson, Principal, 30.
Drama, the, Tennyson's views concerning, 56-61.

Eastbourne, 26.
Education of women, 181.
1809, famous men born in, 1 *note.*
Enoch Arden, 47.
Eyre, Governor, 48.

Farringford, Tennyson's home, 37, 42.
Fitz Gerald, Edward, 1 *note*, 8, 17; criticisms on Tennyson's work and character, 18, 103, 145, 150, 157, 194.
Fletcher, Rev. H., 87.
Frater Ave, 64.
Froude, J. A., 59.

Garibaldi, visit to Tennyson, 46.
Gladstone, W. E., 1 *note*, 52, 66, 67, 68.
Gleam, The, 203.
Goethe, 132.
Grasby, land owned by Tennyson, 26.
Greece, King and Queen of, 67.
Green, J. R., 87.

Hallam, Arthur, at Cambridge, 8; expedition to Spain with Tennyson, 11; engagement to Emily Tennyson, 12; Tennyson's friendship for, 15; death of, 16.

(241)